ar

a guide to contemporary art spaces

•••

kathy battista and siân tichar
photographs by mary barone

art new york

a guide to contemporary art spaces

• • • ellipsis

•••

BRITISH LIBRARY CATALOGUING IN PUBLICATION
A CIP record for this book is available from the British Library

PUBLISHED BY •••ellipsis
2 Rufus Street London N1 6PE
EMAIL ...@ellipsis.co.uk
WWW http://www.ellipsis.com
SERIES EDITOR Tom Neville
SERIES DESIGN Jonathan Moberly

ISBN 1 84166 021 3

PRINTING AND BINDING Hong Kong

For a copy of the Ellipsis catalogue or information on special quantity orders of Ellipsis books please contact our sales manager on 020 7739 3157 or sales@ellipsis.co.uk

Kathy Battista and Siân Tichar 2000

contents

Introduction

Art New York comprises a personal and unashamedly subjective selection of what we believe to be the most influential, historically significant and entertaining galleries dedicated to contemporary art. However, and despite the obvious limitations that are inherent in a book of this scale, we have attempted to present a cross-section of galleries distributed throughout the city and varying in size, style and programme. In addition to providing information on artists represented or shown by each gallery, we have aimed to capture the atmosphere and individual qualities of each space or institution.

In Manhattan alone there are more than 800 commercial galleries, all vying for the most talented artists, lucrative deals and placements in prestigious collections. The past few years have seen the art scene spread outside of Manhattan and certain spaces – such as Pierogi 2000 in Brooklyn and PS1 in Queens– have become compulsory stops on the itineraries of collectors and art lovers alike.

The New York art scene, like art scenes the world over, is vulnerable to whimsies of taste and finance. Shifts and fluctuations in the financial world that funds and allows the art industry to exist directly correlate to its economic situation. One of the most important geographic changes in recent years has resulted in the mass exodus of art galleries from Soho to Chelsea. Soho first became popular as an area frequented by artists and dealers in the 1970s when it was underpopulated, dilapidated and ungentrified. Artists seized on Soho as an affordable area, and they in turn attracted the wealthy individuals who patronise the arts. By the mid 1980s the area was booming as the epicentre of the international art world. Galleries such as Sonnabend, Leo Castelli and Mary Boone ruled the art market, and captured the attention of the media, who burned images of their glamorous lives on to the retinas of people everywhere.

The sophisticated world that Soho became, thanks to the phenomenal success of the galleries located there, led inexorably to an enormous rise in real-estate prices. The disposable incomes of the people visiting Soho quickly attracted the attention of the retail world who set up camp there, converting it to the veritable shopping mall that it is today. What began as the occasional elite boutique has now expanded to feature the chains of stores found in malls across America. Except for a few – Prada, Yamamoto, Anna Sui – the stores cater to the middle-class shopper and range from Victoria's Secret (a very average albeit popular lingerie chain) to Pottery Barn (America's answer to Habitat). Ten years ago encounters with celebrities and the movers and shakers of creative industry were common whilst walking through Soho. Today you are more likely to see New Jersey housewives and their teenage offspring shopping for the latest high-street style.

The majority of galleries that left Soho relocated to the area between 14th and 26th Streets, west of 9th Avenue. Until recently, Chelsea was a derelict, even dangerous, part of town full of warehouses and industrial units. These huge spaces were the ideal size for showing contemporary art and, after some teething problems, Chelsea has become a seething mass of art galleries, artists and art openings. Fashion retail is once again hot on the trail, with the space-age-pod-style Comme des Garçons boutique designed by Future Systems on 22nd Street and a handful of trendy eateries and watering holes conveniently located nearby. Inevitably, Chelsea too will one day be superceded as an art centre, but for the time being it is a hotspot of talent, dealers and dealing.

But the geographical shifts are not limited just to Soho moving to Chelsea. Many influential and inspirational dealers have chosen to remain in Soho (arguably it is those with good-sized space and a level of success that allows them to continue to meet the exorbitant rent requirements). Those newer galleries which could not afford to be there in the first place have started a trend that shows no sign of dissipating, opening up across the river in Brooklyn's Williamsburg. Just as Shoreditch in London's East End was once the only area near the centre of the city where artists could afford to live, so too in Williamsburg self-starting individuals unwittingly add to the value of the area and therefore all that happens there. Ironically, they then have to leave as they can no longer afford the rising cost of living. Williamsburg is still in a state of flux, but its reputation for easily affordable accommodation and studio space is a thing of the past.

The experimental, less price-driven work that can be found in Williamsburg is a million miles away from the high-end dealing going on around 57th Street and in the more prestigious galleries in Soho, Chelsea and Uptown. Undeniably, one of the most exciting parts of New York's art world are the wealthy, influential and shrewd people who comprise this market. Art is subject to fashion, taste and the money markets and consequently the stakes are high. Celebrities from all halls of fame are as apparent on the art scene as blossoming talent. Dealers are desperate to catch a star in the ascendant and the world's press is waiting to pounce on each season's newest comet. It is a ruthless world and only the strong survive. As a result the top players are incredibly successful people whose business acumen and eye for trend spotting are phenomenally inspirational.

New York's art scene is distinguished from others around the world by the personalities who make things happen. The people who dominate both the business and creative sides have become famous in their own right; their stories resulting in books, movies and gossip-column speculation. The names of Ana Mendiata, Andy Warhol, Jean-Michel Basquiat and Valerie Solanas conjure up images of drugs, money, nightclubs and attempted murder. While all of these people are dead, their stories are part of the legendary recent history of the New York art world. The 1980s were particularly notorious years, when prices of work shot up to record highs and the market thrived. Later in the decade the bottom collapsed with the decline of the stock market and many dealers and artists were forced to 'reassess their options'.

Today the market in New York is still dominated by the old guard who previously captured headlines: Mary Boone is highly regarded as was her old partner Leo Castelli and Sonnabend. Alanna Heiss at PS1 has been a force to be reckoned with for the past 20 years, building her institution from one without a home to the gargantuan outpost of MoMA. However, the importance of younger and more accessible dealers should not be underestimated. Matthew Marks, Jack Shainman and Jack Tilton have all cut their teeth on the storm of the art market crash of the late 1980s and persevered with their knack for spotting young talent and capitalising on it. Joe Amrhein of Pierogi 2000 and Marcia Tucker of The Drawing Center have become equally renowned for their commitment to working with artists in a non-profit context. Although not as flamboyant as Marks or Shainman, Amrhein and Tucker are known the world over for bringing important alternative art into the limelight.

There are many spaces in New York dedicated to contemporary art which are worthy of recognition but that we are unable to feature in the book: Peter Blum, Tibor de Nagy and Roebling Hall are among the names that could not be fitted into this first edition of *Art New York*. Other institutions, such as Kunsthalle NY, are in the process of finding new homes and therefore cannot be included. This book is not intended to be prescriptive, instead providing a taster of the intricate and varied art that is on offer in what is arguably the world's leading metropolis. Our best advice is to use it as a starting point, from which to venture forward. Visit one of the galleries, then have a search around the neighbourhood. One of the great things about New York is that it is always changing – some of the galleries in this book may have even moved or closed by the time it is published. New and important spaces may have opened. Whatever the case we found it incredibly satisfying to venture out and discover the myriad riches that comprise the New York art world. We hope that you will do the same.

NOTE

Many of the galleries listed have set up or are in the process of creating websites. Where possible, we have included the addresses in this guide. We recommend viewing these sites, as some of them are incredibly innovative and informative.

Several publications offer listings and time-specific information on the galleries that feature in this book. The *Gallery Guide* published monthly by Art Now is available freely at most galleries, but you may need to request a copy. *Simonsays*, which takes the form of a pamphlet available at some galleries, is a more critical monthly overview, and a swift way of selecting the best that is on offer.

ACKNOWLEDGEMENTS

Kathy and Siân wish to thank Tom Neville and everyone at ellipsis for their support and enthusiasm; Mary Barone for the gorgeous pictures and for going above and beyond the call of duty; Mary Dinaburg and all at Dinaburg Arts for their dedication to the project; Sharon Essor for her help and encouragement.

Kathy wishes to thank Siân for inviting her to become part of this project; Nigel Talamo and Tracey Ferguson for moral support and practical advice; and her family.

Siân wishes to thank Kathy for making this project so enjoyable; Helen Allen and Lilli-Mari Andresen for their wit and wisdom; Richard Kennaugh for his views on contemporary art; and Karel and Liz Ticha.

Mary Barone would especially like to thank Jim Cottrell and Joe Lovett.

tribeca

Ace Gallery New York

If you're not in the know you could easily walk right by this space without realising that a gallery exists here. The façade of Ace Gallery is a brick wall and the only indication that there is anything other than storage behind it is a small plaque near the unassuming entrance.

But visitors should not be fooled: Ace is one of the most incredible gallery spaces in the whole of New York. Its size alone is overwhelming, and the huge spaces it houses in various rooms located off a cavernous hall allow it to show an extraordinarily exciting range of large-scale art and installations. Richard Serra and Tim Hawkinson are among the artists whose massive pieces can be shown to maximum effect within a gallery whose giant proportions give it a more museum-like feel than any other commercial gallery in Manhattan.

Ace also has a reputation for mystery and this proved true when the gallery declined to reveal any more about itself other than that it is owned by Douglas Chrismas, who owns equally spectacular spaces in Los Angeles and Mexico City.

Do not let the lack of information be a deterrent; Ace Gallery is full of surprises and most of them deliver more than satisfying results.

ADDRESS 275 Hudson Street, New York, NY 10013 (212 255 5599)
OPEN Tuesday to Saturday, 10.00–18.00
SUBWAY Canal Street 1, 9

Ace Gallery New York

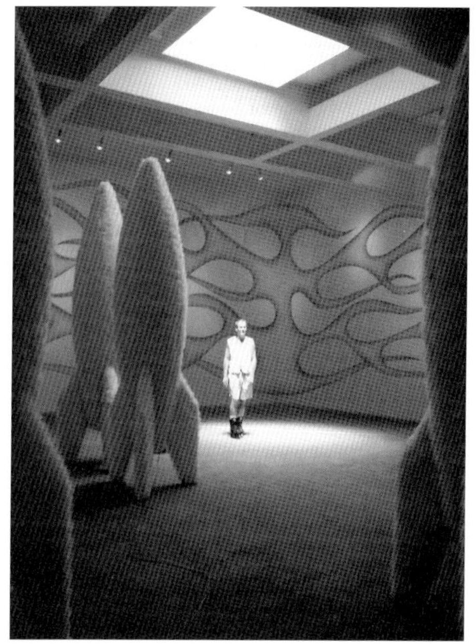

Apex Art C.P.

Although Apex Art C.P. (Curatorial Program) is located on busy Church Street in highly fashionable Tribeca, it maintains a modest profile. The opaque windows of the façade lend a secretive air to the gallery. However, Apex is anything but insular. Founded in 1994 by artist Steven Rand, Apex is a non-profit exhibition space that exists in order to explore a diverse range of issues. Instead of taking the usual route of hiring a curator or taking on the responsibility himself, Rand and his board invite curators to mount idea-based shows. Each of these is accompanied by an expensive-looking pamphlet that includes a scholarly essay by the curator and colour reproductions of works from the exhibition. Collated, these provide a detailed history of the feats which Apex has accomplished.

Apex manages to create a stimulating discourse and to keep the commercial side of the art world out of its affairs; it never engages in sales or sales-related activities and concentrates only on ideas. Besides the curated exhibition programme, Apex also runs a Studio Program that provides residencies for artists. During each term of the project one American artist and two foreign artists are invited to make work in a studio space and live in a shared apartment. The aim of the project is to assemble diverse individuals and to build international relationships by assisting in the development of skills in a new environment. Like the curated shows, each Studio project is commemorated by a classy colour brochure.

Apex Art has worked with some of the most renowned and cutting edge curators from around the world. In this unassuming space a visitor can experience the vision of Hou Hanru, Casey Kaplan, Donald Kuspit, Maria Lind, Michael Toledo, Joshua Decter, Laura Cottingham and Collier Schorr. In addition, Carlos Basualdo co-ordinates Apex Art's International Program, which consists of an annual exhibition that reflects multicultural discourse and takes international issues as its point

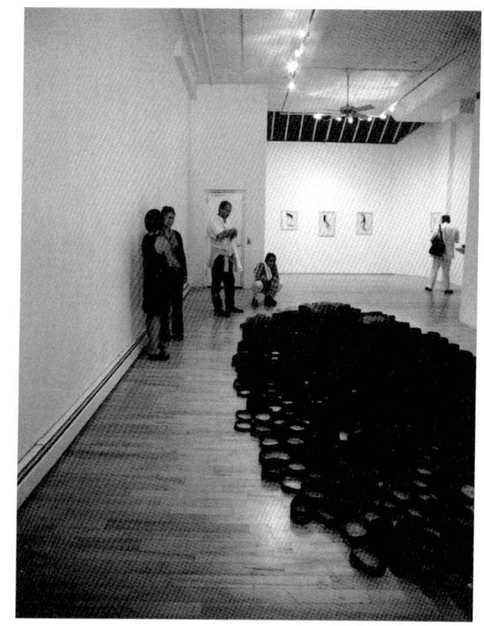

of departure. Like the main exhibition program, the International Program invites curators to mount the shows.

Apex is a dream come true for artists and curators. It attests to the fact that galleries can foster new ideas and create a much-needed critical discussion of contemporary art and issues.

ADDRESS 291 Church Street, New York, NY 10013 (212 431 5270)
WEBSITE www.apexart.org
OPEN Tuesday to Saturday, 11.00–18.00
SUBWAY Franklin Street 1, 9/Canal Street A, C, E

Apex Art C.P.

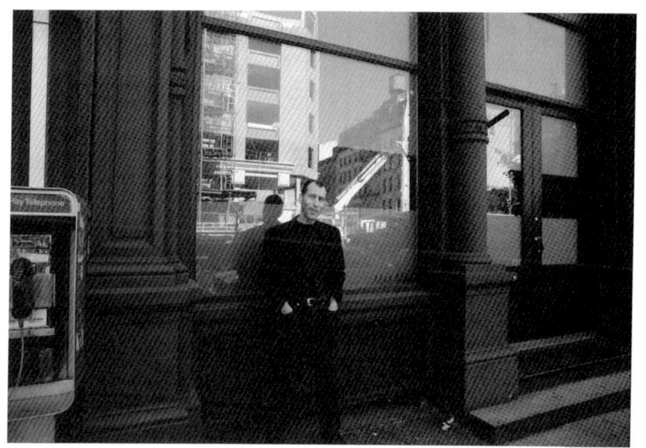

soho

101 Spring Street

One of the most frustrating spaces in which to view contemporary art because you can only peer through the windows, 101 Spring Street is nevertheless a must-see on the Soho art tour. The building was the minimalist maestro Donald Judd's sanctuary in New York. Since his death, it has been managed by his estate. Judd bought the cast-iron building, situated on a right-angle plot, in November 1968, before Soho became a desirable part of town. Like other artists of his generation, including Robert Morris and Richard Serra, Judd bought run-down property that is today worth a small fortune.

Originally built in 1870 by Nicholas Whyte, the five-storey building was in a terrible state when Judd purchased it. The interior had been ruined by heavy machinery and there was so much trash that Judd joked Arman could have bought it and left it as an installation. However, he was attracted to the floorplan:

Donald Judd I thought the building should be repaired and basically not changed. It is a nineteenth-century building. It was pretty certain that each floor should have one purpose: sleeping, eating, working.

Judd kept the interior structure of the building intact and used the open floor plan to his advantage. Each floor provided a working or living environment for the sculptor, but most importantly it provided space in which Judd could install the impressive collection of artwork that he was amassing.

Passers-by can look through the ground-floor windows and identify the work of Carl Andre and Dan Flavin, at one time Judd's closest confidante. At present it contains more work by other artists than by Judd himself, whose ambitions grew too large for the Spring Street location.

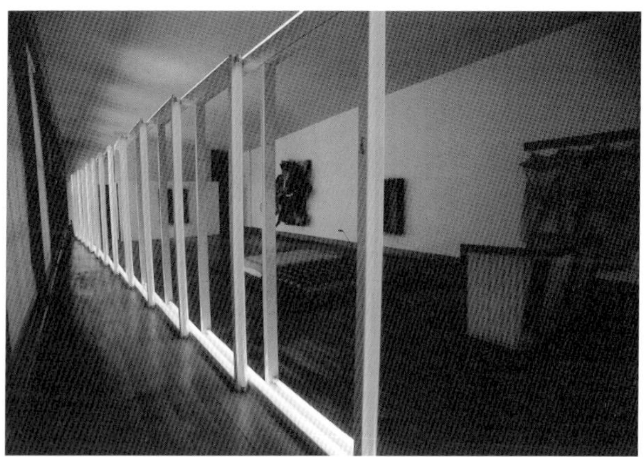

He went on eventually to acquire most of Marfa, a Texan desert town, setting it up as an alternative to museum exhibitions. 101 Spring Street turned out to be only a taster for Judd's eccentric yet enigmatic exhibiting techniques.

ADDRESS 101 Spring Street (corner of Mercer Street), New York, NY 10012
ACCESS none
SUBWAY Prince Street N, R

101 Spring Street

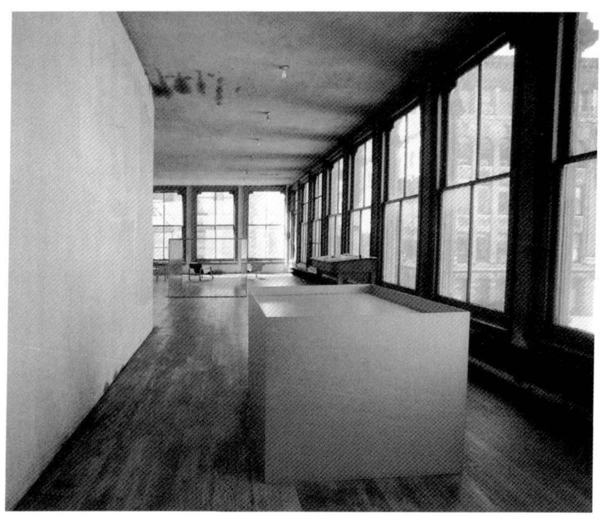

American Fine Arts

Colin Deland is the man behind American Fine Arts and has been a player in the New York art world for two decades. He is part of the group responsible for the naissance of the Armory Art Show that includes respected contemporary dealers Pat Hearn, Mathew Marks and Paul Morris (Deland is also the husband of Hearn).

American Fine Arts shows a variety of work including installation, drawing, painting and sculpture by emerging and more established contemporary artists. Deland showed John Water's *Director's Cut* at his gallery in 1996 to rave reviews and regularly uses his space to expand the discourse on the aesthetics of art. The 1998 exhibition by Crowd of Women, *Collection of Frank Schroder 1909–1959*, consisted of 90 paintings by various artists collected from flea markets and auctions. Another eccentric showcase took place two years earlier. *Fantastic Sh*t* featured large silkscreeen illustrations that had to be viewed with 3-D glasses.

Although New York's art world seems to be dominated by blue-chip dealers, Colin Deland provides a refreshing alternative. While he has been on the scene for a very long time, he has retained the ability to surprise.

ADDRESS 22 Wooster Street, New York, NY 10012 (212 941 0401)
OPEN Tuesday to Saturday, 12.00–18.00
SUBWAY Canal Street A, C, E

American Fine Arts

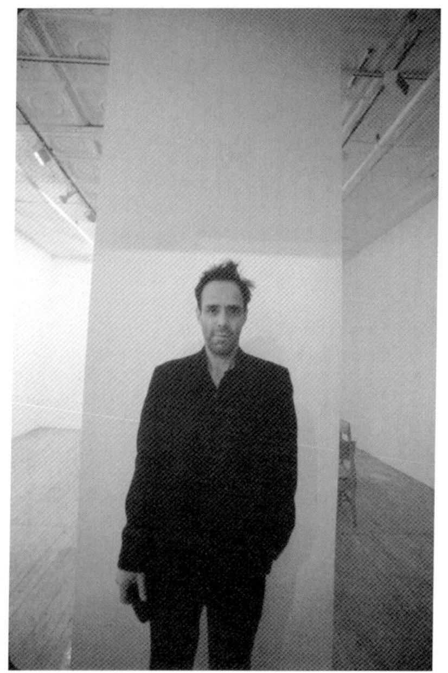

Artists Space

The first artist-run space to be funded by the state council, Artists Space is renowned for its egalitarian attitude towards its curatorial programme. It was founded in 1973 as a not-for-profit institution supporting contemporary art and artists in the visual arts including video, performance, architecture and design. Since then it seems that everyone who is anyone in New York's art world – artist, curator, or dealer – has at one time or another participated in a project connected to Artists Space.

This was exemplified in a publication commemorating its 25th anniversary that was brought out in 1999. Everyone – from Ann Hamilton and Hudson to Barbara Kruger, Frank Gehry and Nan Goldin –contributed their comments on the space and their involvement with it in *5000 Artists Return to Artists Space: 25 Years*. It is an impressive testament to the scope and range of activities here, plus the countless careers that have been springboarded through the gallery.

Democratic almost to a fault, the policy of choosing which artists are given the opportunity to exhibit at Artists Space always comes down to a rigorous voting procedure. Initially a panel of prominent people in the visual arts in New York State – administrators, critics and artists such as George Segal and Jeff Way – were asked what it was that the art world needed at that time aside from grants to individual artists.

After they had moved into the first site at the corner of Wooster and Houston Streets (they spent that summer cleaning the space with the help of local artists and Philip Glass even came along to offer his services as a plumber) the committee drew up a list of 21 well-known artists to cover nine months of one-person shows. Chuck Close, Donald Judd, Vito Acconci, Sol LeWitt, Richard Serra and Nancy Graves were among those invited to choose one unaffiliated artist. When works were sold all proceeds went to the artist.

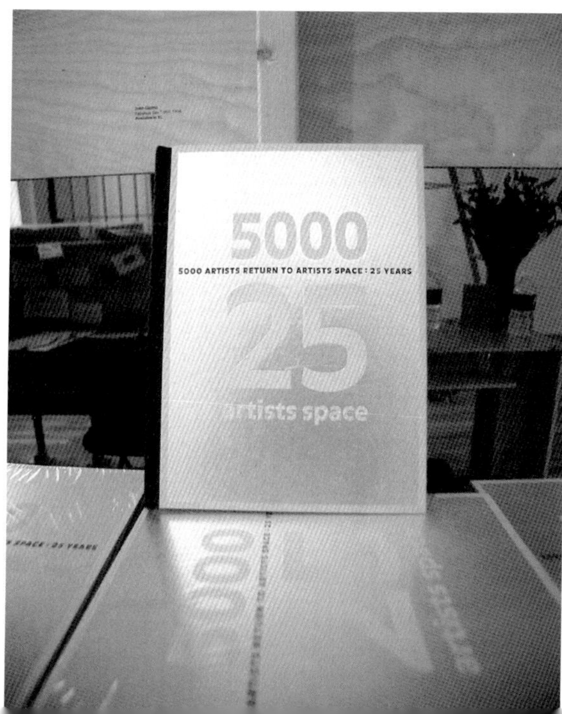
5000
5000 ARTISTS RETURN TO ARTISTS SPACE : 25 YEARS
25
artists space

Artists Space

Artists Space is also home to The Irving Sandler Artists File. Sandler was the first board president until 1980. The artists file bearing his name is a digitised image database and slide registry that is open to the public free of charge. It is regularly used by curators, artists, gallery owners, collectors, consultants and students to view the work of emerging and unaffiliated artists. With Artists Space's connections it is hardly surprising that their file is one of the largest and most comprehensive artist registries in the country. Artists submit applications to be considered for inclusion in the files. Once in the system they must update their material every year or two. This was the model for many other schemes of this sort, such as Pierogi 2000 in Williamsburg and Mary Jane Aladren's Nylon in London.

Certain artists' files can be accessed via the website. Each month a selection of artists from the files is presented to viewers. One can look at examples of their work without having to travel to the gallery. Biographies and resumes are also included for each artist.

Now in its late 20s, it could be argued that Artists Space has become more mature and definitely more established. It was once the kind of place where an evening of poetry reading turned into an all night sit-in, with gallery staff returning the next morning to find that visitors had never gone home. You are unlikely to experience this type of occurrence today but for those lucky enough to have been there, there were moments that will certainly never be forgotten.

ADDRESS 38 Greene Street, New York, NY 10013 (212 226 3970)
WEBSITE www.artistsspace.org
OPEN Tuesday to Saturday, 10.00–18.00
SUBWAY Spring Street C, E

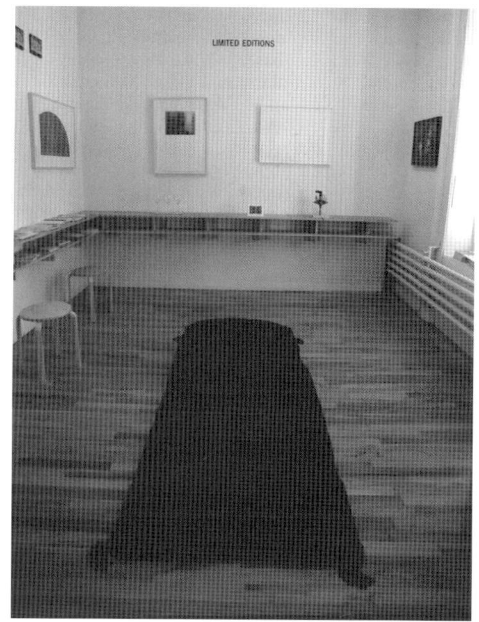
LIMITED EDITIONS

Marianne Boesky Gallery

If the name of this gallery sounds familiar to you, your hunch is probably correct. Marianne Boesky is the daughter of that infamous risk arbitrageur of Wall Street, Ivan Boesky. While her father found himself in federal prison, Marianne seems destined for notoriety for smaller deals.

Boesky represents many young artists and, at 33, is quite young herself. Holding a law degree, Boesky appears to have a grounded perspective on the art market. While understanding that it is inextricably bound to Wall Street, Boesky asserts that you cannot buy works of art for investment; only for love.

Boesky carries Karin Davie, Sarah Sze, and Lisa Yuskavage on her books. Like the rest of the Generation X gang, some of her ten artists have an irreverent attitude towards the medium used in creating their art. Yet many of them do continue to work on canvas and paper. Boesky is aware that work in film and video really only has retail potential on the institutional circuit but she is still willing to represent people who produce exciting pieces using these forms.

Perhaps unsurprisingly, Boesky rarely sells to people walking in off the street, preferring instead to establish relationships with serious collectors in order to place the work of art in 'the right hands'. This attitude may serve to authenticate her integrity as a dealer, and one can only wait to see if it also fulfills her potential as a commercial gallery operator.

ADDRESS 51 Greene Street, New York, NY 10013 (212 941 9888)
OPEN Tuesday to Saturday, 10.00–18.00
SUBWAY Prince Street N, R

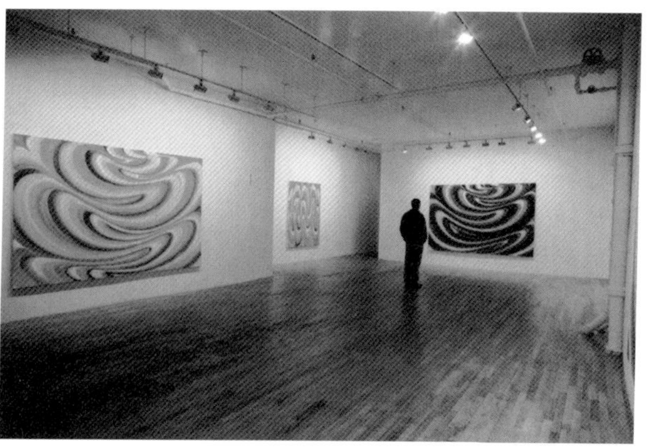

The Broken Kilometer

2.14 On long-term view since 1979 this installation conceived by land artist Walter De Maria consists of 500 highly polished, round, solid brass rods each measuring 2 metres in length and 5 centimetres in diameter. The rods are placed in five parallel rows of 100 rods each. Both this space and The Earth Room are outposts of DIA Center for the Arts (see page 4.10).

This work is the companion piece to De Maria's 1977 'Vertical Earth Kilometer' at Kassel in Germany, where the international art exhibition *Documenta* is held every five years. In that permanently installed earth sculpture a brass rod of the same diameter, total weight, and total length has been inserted 1000 metres into the ground.

Unusual, but unmissable.

ADDRESS 393 West Broadway, New York, NY 10012 (212 925 9397)
WEBSITE www.diacenter.org
OPEN Wednesday to Saturday, 12.00-18.00
SUBWAY Spring Street C, E

The Broken Kilometer

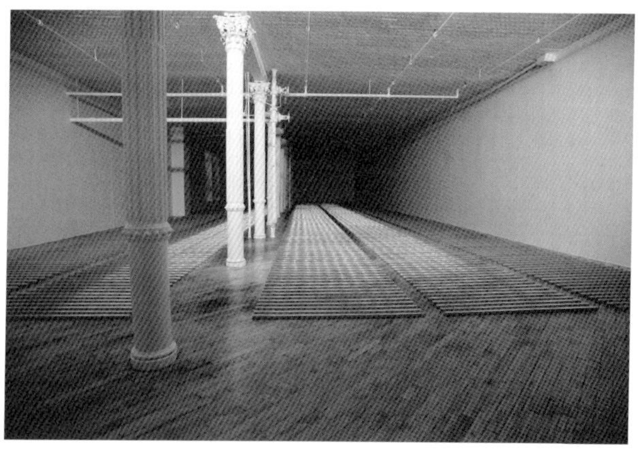

soho

Deitch Projects

Squirreled away on Grand Street, it is easy to stroll past Deitch Projects without even noticing it. But this would be a mistake because Jeffrey Deitch – the man behind the 'projects' – has made a name for himself as a presenter of ambitious work by emerging artists. What this means for the viewer is that a visit to his space often results in a sensory experience of the kind that some more established and commercial galleries might not risk.

Colour, vibrancy, energy and sound are factors that make Deitch Projects worth seeking out. Deitch's artists are, of course, responsible for these vibes and names such as Japanese super-starlet Mariko Mori, Vanessa Beecroft, Barry McGee and Shahzia Sikander certainly explain why. The gallery evokes an international and sometimes ethnic feel – the artists represented originate from more than 20 different countries. But Deitch himself is no stranger to the cosmopolitan prospects of the art world. He has been dealing since 1972 and curated many groundbreaking exhibitions in that time.

Deitch has recently opened an adjunct space across the street from the gallery. Be sure to check out both places.

ADDRESS 76 Grand Street, New York, NY 10013 (212 343 7300)
OPEN Tuesday to Saturday, 12.00–18.00
SUBWAY Spring Street C, E

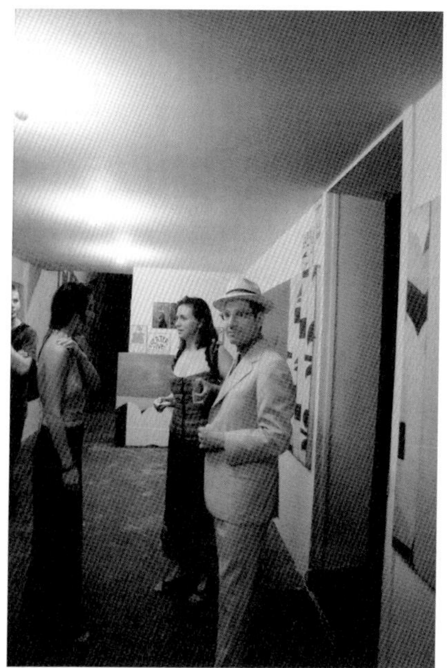

The Drawing Center

Since its establishment by Martha Beck in 1976, The Drawing Center has presented the drawings of more than 1800 emerging artists. In addition to work by new artists, The Drawing Center has shown Old Master drawings by, among others, Michelangelo, Rembrandt, Guercino, Picasso and Redon. This is a tough act to follow for Catherine de Zegher, the latest executive director (appointed in February 1999). Her predecessor, Ann Philben, left The Drawing Center to become director of The Armand Hammer Museum of Art and Cultural Center at UCLA in Los Angeles. De Zegher is only the third director in the Center's 23-year history. She was previously co-founder and director of the Kanaal Art Foundation in Kortrijk, Belgium.

The Drawing Center is the only not-for-profit institution in the USA to focus on exhibiting both contemporary and historic drawings. The space was created in order to provide opportunities for emerging and under-recognised artists to demonstrate the significance of drawing throughout history and to stimulate public dialogue on issues of art and culture.

The Center also actively encourages interaction between artists and visitors by hosting monthly reading events under the banner of 'Nightlight'. Dedicated to presenting new writing in all forms, 'Nightlight's' evening events invite the public to listen to the auspicious likes of Paul Auster, Edward Albee, Fran Lebowitz and George Plimpton reading their work in a relaxed rather than academic atmosphere. The success of this series has more recently resulted in the occasional afternoon reading, 'Nightlight for Kids', which has featured ex-Velvet Underground member John Cale reading an original story for children.

Located on the ground floor of a beautifully restored cast-iron building in Soho, The Drawing Center has the appearance of a small museum rather

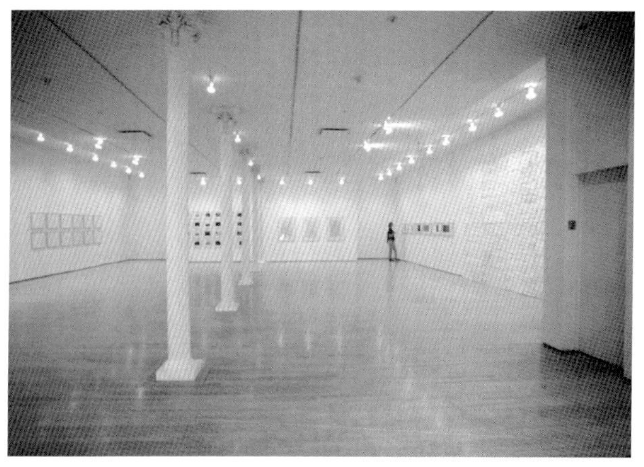

than a gallery. Once inside, a small reception area leads to an open-plan 3100-square-foot gallery space with 13-foot ceilings and red oak floors. A smaller space that features a garage door as its façade is located directly across the street on Wooster; The Project Room is dedicated to site-specific and project-based work. This building also houses the room where gallery staff meet with young artists to review their portfolios.

The Drawing Center has always offered The Viewing Program, an opportunity for artists to have their work reviewed by a member of the curatorial staff. Artists are reviewed on the basis of slides and a resumé . After meeting with a curator from The Center some of the artists are selected to be included in *Selections*, a series of group shows of artists chosen through The Viewing Program. This practice makes the Center unique in its commitment to encouraging artists who have not yet been discovered. A slide registry, which holds more than 5000 images, serves as documentation of the artists that participate in The Viewing Program. Curators, art dealers, and collectors from around the country and abroad frequently consult this file.

In conjunction with each exhibition, The Drawing Center publishes a catalogue that provides a visual and contextual record of the show. These publications range from compact books to large folios. Extremely well put together, the catalogues are must-haves for bibliophiles and stand as testaments to the important work being done by this institution.

ADDRESS 35 Wooster Street, New York, NY 10013 (212 219 2166)
OPEN Tuesday, Thursday, Friday, 10.00–18.00; Wednesday, 10.00–20.00; Saturday, 11.00–18.00
SUBWAY Canal Street A, C, E

The Drawing Center

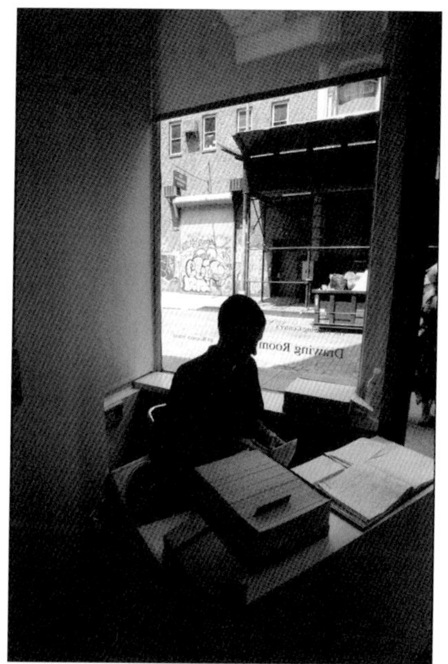

The Earth Room

2.22

Walter De Maria's interior earth sculpture has been on permanent view since 1980.

250 cubic yards of earth
3600 square feet of floor space
22-inch depth of material
Total weight of sculpture 280,000 lbs

Dive in.

ADDRESS 141 Wooster Street, New York, NY 10012 (212 473 8072)
WEBSITE www.diacenter.org
OPEN Wednesday to Saturday, 12.00-18.00
SUBWAY Spring Street C, E

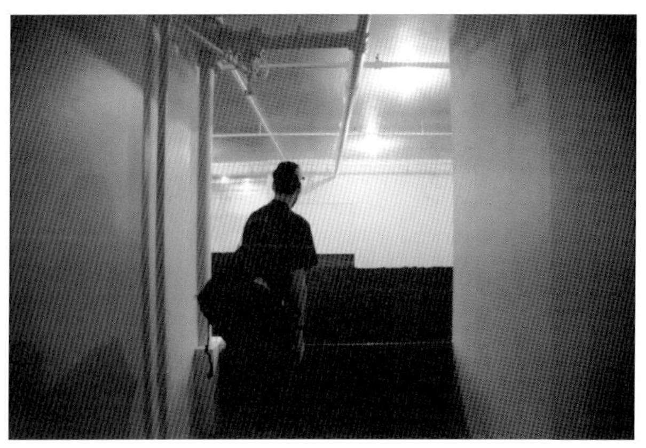

Exit Art

Hugely unmissable and at 17,000 square feet unmissably huge, Exit Art is a space that represents New York's claim to be the epicentre of the contemporary art world. Since its founding in 1982, this not-for-profit organisation has played a significant role as an interdisciplinary laboratory for contemporary culture. Conceivers Jeanette Ingberman and Papo Colo set up Exit Art primarily to present the work of young and emerging artists in context. This policy has allowed the gallery to launch the careers of many now-famous artists: David Hammons, Adrian Piper, David Wojnarowicz and Jimmie Durham are a few names on the extensive list. Exit Art also encourages the exploration of interdisciplinary exchange by playing host to visual art and design, performance, theatre, film, video, music and poetry events.

The organisation fosters creative exchange and collaboration with an open, on-going artist slide review, ready access to directors and staff and a diverse range of readings, panel, discussions and performances which promote interaction and allow creative people to meet and share ideas.

Since 1995 Exit Art has produced an annual limited-edition portfolio of prints by contemporary artists (including Roxy Paine, Nancy Spero, Sean Mellyn, Nicole Eisenman and Tom Otterness). These books have established the presence of Exit Art in the print community and given further exposure to the artists it supports.

ADDRESS 548 Broadway, NY 10012 (212 966 7745)
WEBSITE www.exitart.org
OPEN Tuesday to Thursday, 10.00–18.00; Friday, 10.00–20.00; Saturday, 11.00–18.00
SUBWAY Prince Street N, R

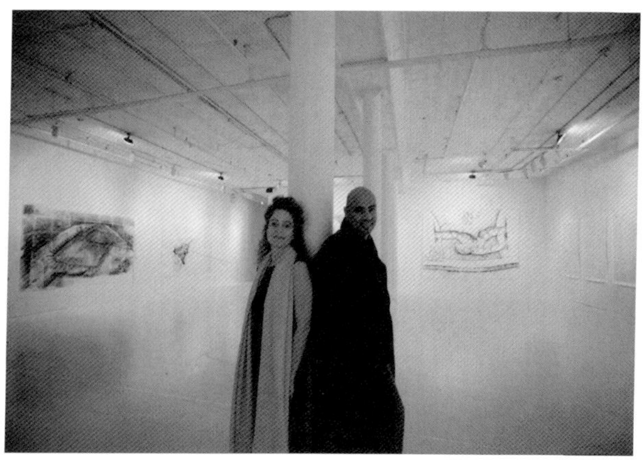

Gagosian Gallery

Larry Gagosian is the formidable presence behind the eponymous uptown and downtown galleries. His career in dealing began in Los Angeles in 1985, then developed in New York where he opened a space on West 23rd Street, between Tenth and Eleventh Avenues, long before the Dia Center or any other galleries existed in that area. In 1988 he moved to his present uptown location on 980 Madison Avenue, which now occupies two floors of the building. But the fact that it is located on the upper floors of what is really an office block made it a very difficult space in which to show larger works. For this reason in November 1991 Gagosian opened a second space on Wooster Street, which was launched with a Richard Serra exhibition. The downtown gallery resembles an industrial space, occupying the street level only. In fact the extremely wide frontage is a massive garage door that revolves upwards, in and out, allowing for difficult and large works to be directly installed into the gallery by truck or crane. This makes it perfect for showing works by gallery artists Walter De Maria, Anselm Kiefer and, of course, Richard Serra.

While Larry Gagosian is the driving force behind the operations, Elan Wingate is the charming and affable director of the downtown space. After running the legendary Sonnabend Gallery in the 1970s, where he worked with artists such as Gilbert & George, he temporarily retired from the art world to work in his family business. In 1987 he re-entered the art scene as a partner in the Koury Wingate Gallery. But this closed in 1991 and he has been director of Gagosian downtown ever since.

Both Gagosians represent the blue-chip side of the art market, holding a veritable who's who of the international art world. Francesco Clemente, Damien Hirst, Annette Messager, Ed Ruscha, David Salle, and Cy Twombly are among those represented by Gagosian Gallery. In addition,

Gagosian Gallery

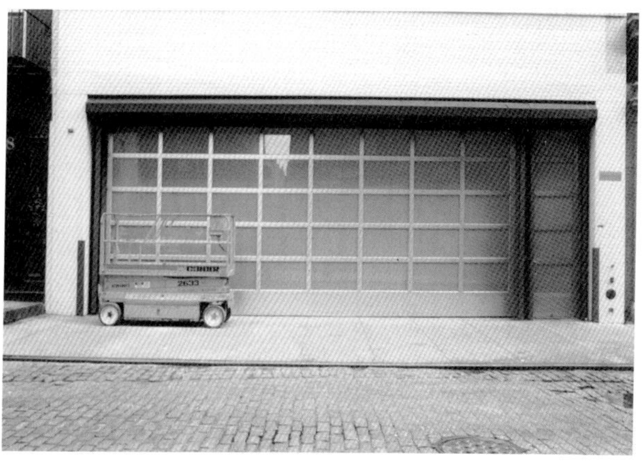

some younger artists such as Cecily Brown and Douglas Gordon complement the lineup. Gagosian is also the only gallery outside of the Saatchi Collection in London permitted to show Jenny Saville's paintings.

The massive scale of the gallery can be intimidating, and so it should be. Here you are entering the highest echelon of the New York art world.

ADDRESS 136 Wooster Street, New York, NY 10012 (212 228 2828)
OPEN Tuesday to Saturday, 10.00–18.00
SUBWAY Prince Street N, R

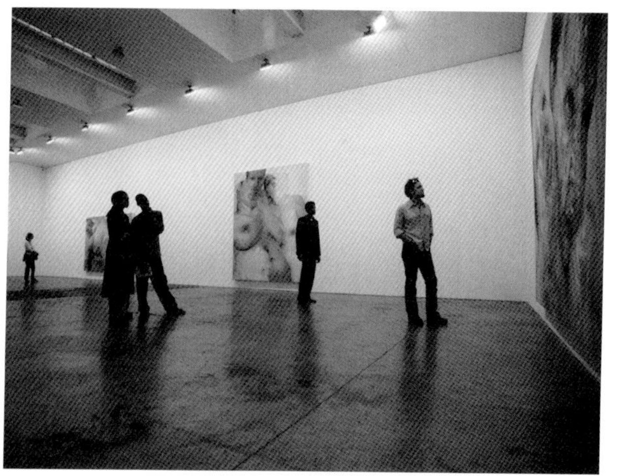

The Hugo Boss Prize at the Guggenheim Museum Soho

This is the platform that launches artists who are not yet household names into the public conscious. Held biannually, The Hugo Boss Prize's official line is an event that recognises outstanding achievement in contemporary art. In reality it is an opportunity to introduce the latest art-world darlings to the masses.

The $50,000 award scheme was started in 1996 and, unlike other international art prizes, does not discriminate by age, nationality or gender. The nominees are chosen on the basis of their entire careers rather than a handful of submitted works. Thus, the exhibition only represents the tip of the iceberg in regard to each of the artists' œuvres.

The prize is the result of a long-term collaboration, begun in 1995, with the German fashion company Hugo Boss. In addition to the biannual event, Boss is a regular sponsor of exhibitions at the Guggenheim which have included *Georg Baselitz*, *Ross Bleckner*, *Ellsworth Kelly*, *Robert Rauschenberg* and *Peggy Guggenheim: A Centennial Celebration*. This sponsorship deal is another example of a corporate identity obtaining integral exposure through supporting the arts. While the financial support is invaluable to the institution, it is only nominal in relation to the amount of brand placement that sponsors demand.

The first Hugo Boss Prize was awarded to Matthew Barney in 1996. Represented by Barbara Gladstone, Barney was a football player at the Ivy League Yale University before turning his hand to installation and video. His Cremaster series is widely popular, blending beautiful imagery with hybrid characters, such as cheerleaders from outer space and Barney as a goat/satyr who tap dances. Barney was in good company for the prize, winning over older and more-established artists such as Laurie Anderson, Stan Douglas and Janine Antoni.The second Hugo Boss Prize, awarded

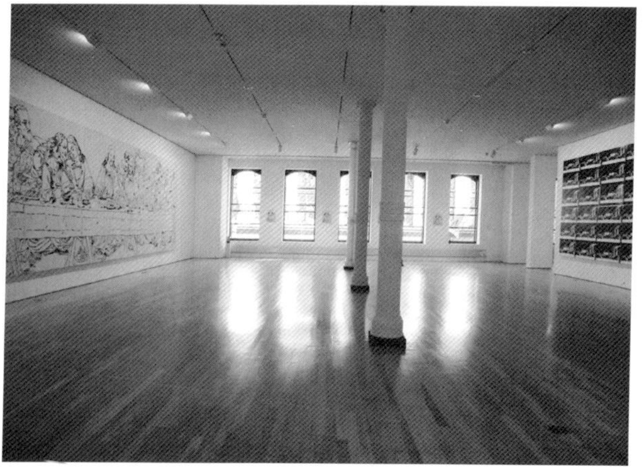

in 1998, went to Scottish artist Douglas Gordon. Known for making work derived from feature films, Gordon showed 'Hysteria' in the exhibition. This piece used turn-of-the-century footage of mental patients, all female, being 'treated' by an attending psychoanalyst, Charcot. Gordon's work was chosen over Chinese artist Yuan Yong Ping, South African William Kentbridge and Swiss artist Pippilotti Rist. 'Sip My Ocean', Rist's seductive video work set to the soundtrack of her squealing Chris Isaak's 'I Don't Want to Fall in Love', was made in the Red Sea. The rich colours of various objects sinking through the water contrasted with Rist's milky white body to create a mesmerising sensation.

The Guggenheim Museum in Soho – often known as the downtown Guggenheim – was only opened in 1992, 33 years after the inaugural exhibition at its big-brother-uptown, the Solomon R Guggenheim Museum designed by visionary architect Frank Lloyd Wright. Since then the downtown Guggenheim has exhibited numerous groundbreaking and popular shows. Its location on busy Broadway places it perfectly for catching flocks of shoppers who might normally be intimidated by the thought of viewing modern or contemporary art.

Rumours are afoot that there may be a new Guggenheim in development, to be located midtown on the West Side Highway. Watch that space!

ADDRESS 575 Broadway, New York, NY 10012 (212 423 3500)
WEBSITE www.guggenheim.org
OPEN Wednesday to Friday, 11.00–18.00; Saturday, 11.00–20.00
SUBWAY Prince Street N, R

The Hugo Boss Prize at the Guggenheim Museum Soho

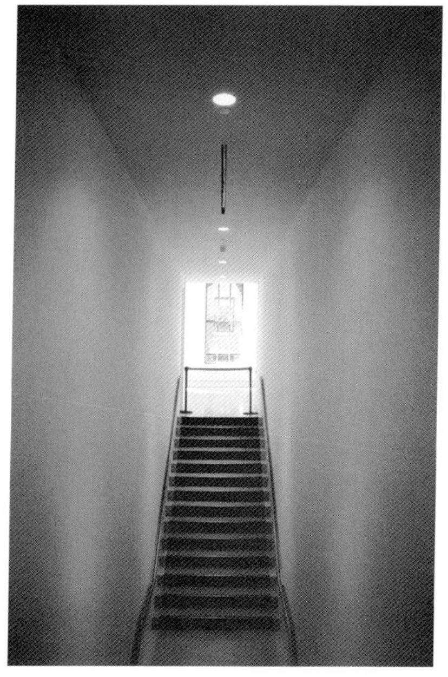

Bronwyn Keenan Gallery

With her waif-like-super-model looks, Bronwyn Keenan does not resemble what you might imagine an ex-Christie's gal to be. But she is. Having spent three years working in the American Paintings department, she left to manage a contemporary art gallery in Soho. For the past five years she has had her own space, the Bronwyn Keenan Gallery (abbreviated to BKG), originally on Broadway but on Crosby Street since 1997.

The artists that she currently represents reflect the air of cutting-edge cool that Keenan herself exudes. One of them, conceptual artist John Hansel, is also the lead singer of hybrid rock band Bianca, which BKG also manages. This glam-kitsch group began as an extension of Hansel's art; his 1998 exhibition combined performance with paraphernalia associated with the band (posters, T-shirts, stickers). Ironically, Bianca was very well received and has subsequently done the rounds of NYC's club circuit, (Limelight, Don Hill's, Life). Hansel is also behind the monthly 'Johnny's Rock'n'Roll Paradise' at Don Hill's, as well as the website www.biancayeah.com.

Sharing information through the worldwide web is something that BKG is devoting time to. Spring 1999 saw the launch of artnewyork.com. The site exists as a community of galleries, artists and writers and is also supported by other local galleries such as Greene Naftali, Gavin Brown's Enterprise and Feature Inc., and has a partnership with amazon.com. It is worth checking out for exhibition reviews, gossip and The Shop, a lower-end product line where you can buy limited-edition pieces from artists.

The other artists at BKG also seem to have a unique flair for attracting interest. Reverend Ethan Acres debuted in New York with the millennium exhibition at the gallery. *Reverend Acres Rockin' Millennium Countdown* took as its starting point the Four Horsemen of the Apocalypse and

Bronwyn Keenan Gallery

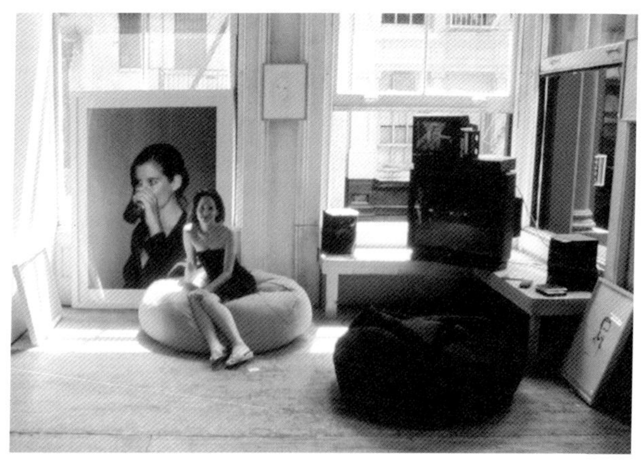

combined sculpture, painting and performance. Keenan also exhibited photographer Michael Seymour's never-before-seen photos of Terence Stamp, Michael Caine and Julie Christie, among others, in 1960s London. Primarily known for his work in production design (he won a BAFTA and was nominated for an Oscar for his involvement in *Alien*), Seymour had also worked as a paparazzo and photographer for *Scene Magazine*. Fourteen of those photos were recently purchased by the National Portrait Gallery in London.

Bronwyn Keenan Gallery, like Keenan herself, and the scene she is part of and for which she is partly responsible, is one to watch and definitely one to visit.

ADDRESS 3 Crosby Street, New York, NY 10013 (212 431 5083)
WEBSITE www.artnewyork.com
OPEN Tuesday to Saturday, 11.00–18.00
SUBWAY Broadway N, R

Bronwyn Keenan Gallery

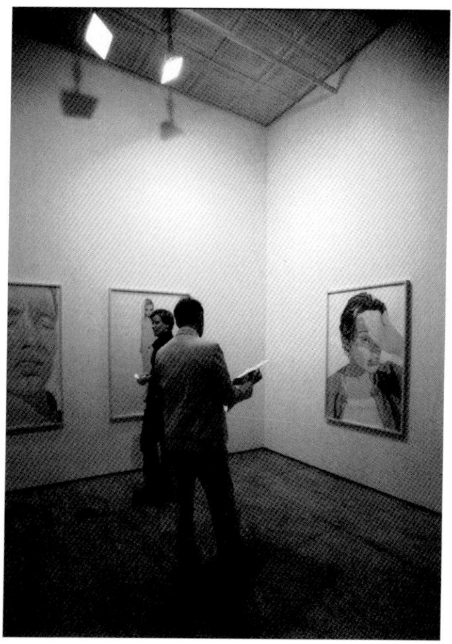

Sean Kelly

Striking. Minimal. Powerful. Unique. Not the gallery, but the man himself. Striking in appearance, Kelly is minimalist in his style of dressing and minimal in terms of hair. His power lies in his ability to secure positions for the work of his artists in important private and public collections. And he maintains a uniquely evolved relationships with the 13 artists that he represents.

SK I watch and wait in order to ascertain who is available when. I have noticed a trend that good artists often leave their first dealers between the ages of 35 and 45. That's when I become interested in them. If I believe in their longevity and providing they are willing to commit to a stable relationship with the gallery I take them on.

Kelly's understanding of artists' needs stems from his own training as one. In his native England his first job on the administrative side of the art world was as director of art for the Bath Festival. Believing that one shouldn't stay in a public position for longer than five or six years, when offered a directorship of a new gallery in New York, Kelly jumped at the opportunity. It was the end of the 1980s and the art market was booming. Kelly's introduction to New York came at an exciting time; after three years he set up on his own, taking artists Ann Hamilton and Marina Abramovic with him.

In the beginning he worked privately out of his loft in Soho. 'I wanted to do things that were not in line with the general mould of dealers and galleries. And I found that there was a hunger and need for what I was doing.' So much so that his wife, Mary Kelly, soon became tired of the non-stop stream of collectors and curators that were passing through the apartment. It was a lucky coincidence that Kelly found the current Mercer

Sean Kelly

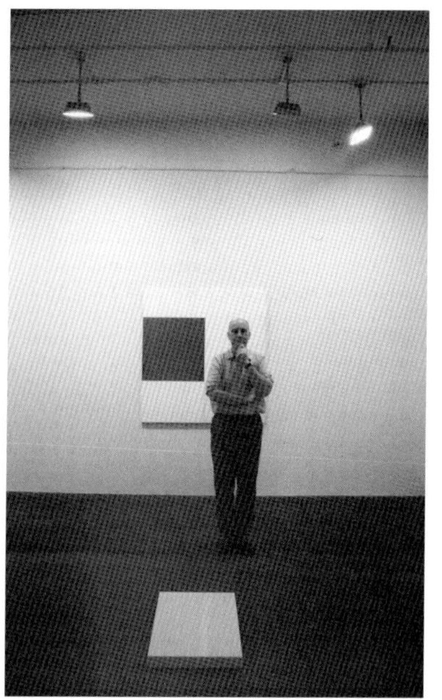

soho

Street location as he was walking by one day. The unassuming façade opens into a large sloping rectangular space. Originally intended only as an office, necessity turned it into a gallery. In 1995 Sean Kelly became the first commercial space to open in Soho after the recession. The inaugural show by Lorna Simpson was covered by PBS who were shooting a documentary on her at the time and their presence fuelled the furor created by the opening.

Kelly sees his role less as a dealer and more as a producer – plotting and planning his artist's careers. He has fostered Marina Abramovic, from never having shown in New York to winning the prize at the 1997 Venice Biennale. For two years Lorna Simpson and Laurie Anderson were finalists in the Hugo Boss prize. Cathy de Monchaux and Christine Borland were selected as candidates for the Tate Gallery's prestigious Turner Prize. In 1999, under Kelly's supervision, Ann Hamilton occupied the American Pavilion at the Venice Biennale. Obviously the calibre of Kelly's artists is excellent; however, his role in supporting and promoting their work cannot be underestimated.

Two-thirds of the artists represented are female (when questioned, Kelly asserts that work is selected on the basis of talent rather than gender). Not that his male artists are floundering in their wake; Callum Innes won the 1998 NatWest Art Prize and James Casabere, Juliao Sarmento and Thomas Joshua Cooper have all won prizes or been bestowed with honours.

ADDRESS 43 Mercer Street, New York, NY 10013 (212 343 2405)
WEBSITE www.skny.com
OPEN Tuesday to Saturday, 11.00–18.00
SUBWAY Canal Street N, R

Sean Kelly

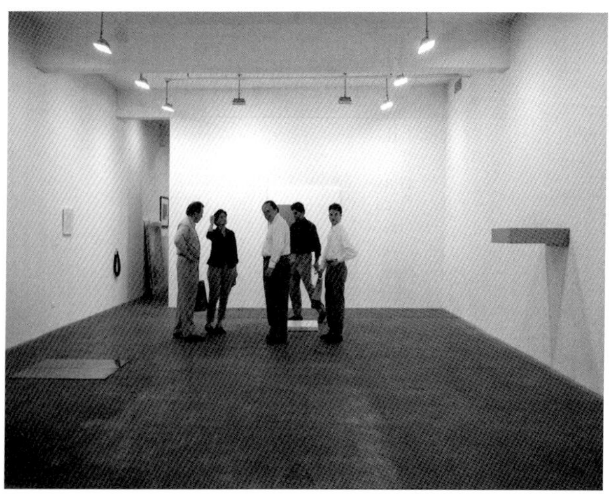

2.42

Anna Kustera Gallery

Set back from the storefronts of Wooster Street, what is now Anna Kustera Gallery used to be the trendy 1980s restaurant Cinco de Mayo. The split levels of the space attest to its exciting history as a place to be seen, and allow Anna to accommodate a variety of work. Kustera, who was director of Josh Baer and also worked for the artist Robert Longo and Artists Space, opened this, her first gallery, in 1996.

Kustera represents an eclectic range of young talent who use a wide variety of media. Sean Mellyn, the painter who attaches large prosthetic body parts to colour-saturated, meticulously realised paintings of children, has found success through her gallery. So too has David Craven, whose paintings are rife with protrusions and bulbous forms.

Some of Kustera's artists also work in video and sculpture. Amy Jenkins makes videos that are projected on to tiny objects; for example a projection of a nude couple sleeping on a dollhouse bed. Daniela Dooling uses personal narrative to create sculptures about female identity that are incorporated into videos. For one piece she has sewn thousands of artificial nails on to a straitjacket to reflect a period of her life when drug-induced mental illness resulted in Dooling incessantly scratched at her flesh with her own nails. Photographs and a video document the artist wearing the piece, which was later exhibited in the windows of Saks Fifth Avenue. Dooling went on to seek funding to create a Prozac gown, made from the real tablets (her drug fascination moving with the times!). Kustera's ability to find a range of talent marks her out as a gallery dealer whose artists are definitely worth watching.

ADDRESS 41 Wooster Street, New York, NY 10013 (212 965 1527)
OPEN Tuesday to Saturday, 10.00–18.00
SUBWAY Canal Street A, C, E

Anna Kustera Gallery

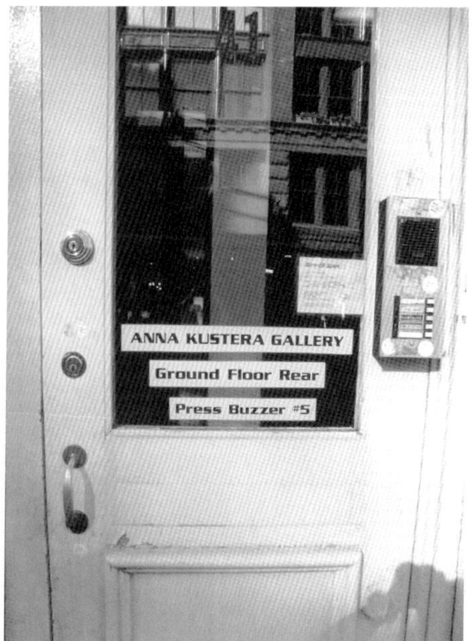

Lehmann Maupin

Directors Rachel Lehmann and David Maupin have something significant to boast about – theirs is the only completed space in the United States designed by Dutch *uber*-architect Rem Koolhaas. International acclaim, book deals, and a jet-set lifestyle more like that of a pop star than an architect make Koolhaas the Buddha of the architectural world. So how did they get him?

David Maupin had been working as director of the Manhattan gallery Metro Pictures (see page 4.46). When Rem Koolhaas needed advice on contemporary American artists, he approached the gallery, and a friendship ensued. Maupin had been associated with Rachel Lehmann through a collaboration between Metro Pictures and Galerie Lehmann that resulted in the temporary Offshore Gallery in Easthampton, Long Island. (The Eritrean-born, German- and Swiss-educated Lehmann had been operating galleries in Geneva and Lausanne.)

Lehmann and Maupin found they shared a common understanding of what a post-1980s gallery should encompass. A belief that an exhibition space should be responsive to the needs of many individuals – artists, collectors, curators, and critics – led to their decision to open a space together. Once they decided to do so, they asked Koolhaas for advice on the design. The organic nature of the affair should not be underestimated as for the past 20 years Koolhaas has turned down many offers to design in the United States and abroad.

The gallery is actually quite similar to other spaces that show art in Soho. The only major intervention Koolhaas made was adding two 16-foot-tall walls on rollers. These divide the space into two halves, the street side being a more traditional gallery space while the rear section uses an impressive skylight to provide dramatic natural light. Koolhaas' design was intended to create a space where artists can change the conditions

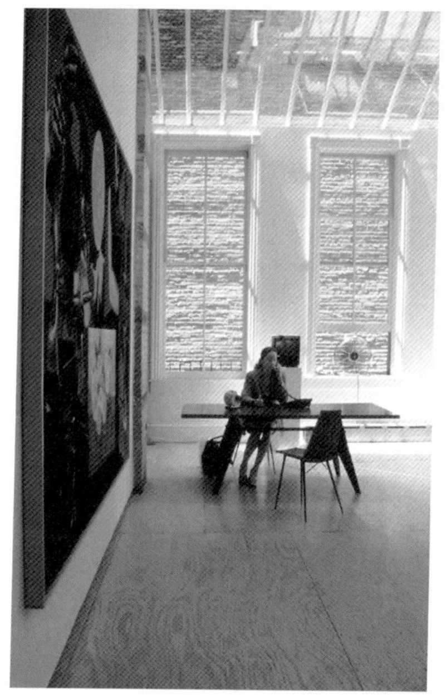

of exhibiting: painting the plywood floors, altering the ceiling, moving walls. Flexibility, rather than definite building form, is the key design issue.

Moving Pictures, the inaugural show in October 1996 at Lehmann Maupin, featured a life-sized sculpture of an elevator by Richard Artschwager and voice-operated light-bulbs by Tony Oursler. Since then they have had a combination of curated and more traditional solo shows. For example, *The Crystal Stopper* was a group show curated by Carlos Basualdo on the theme of the mirror, a virtual *leitmotif* for cultural identity. The walls of the gallery have also been graced by Ross Bleckner, Mike Kelley, Jeff Koons and Terry Winters. Events such as a poetry reading by the current *enfant terrible* Tracey Emin is testament to the diversity of activity supported by the gallery.

ADDRESS 39 Greene Street, New York, NY 10013 (212 965 0753)
OPEN Tuesday to Saturday, 10.00–18.00
SUBWAY Prince Street N, R

Lehmann Maupin

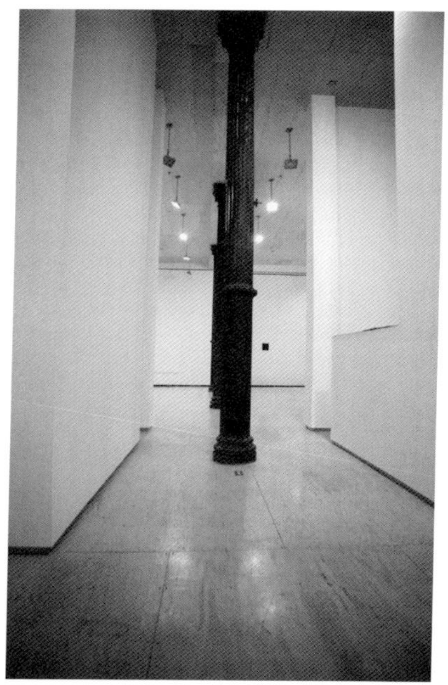

soho

New Museum of Contemporary Art

Entering the New Museum of Contemporary Art is an experience that can only be compared to riding a roller coaster for the first time. It is guaranteed to thrill, shock, and sometimes delight but always exhilarate and inspire those who take the time to explore all that goes on behind its glass façade.

Founded in an office on Hudson Street in the Lower East Side in 1977 by Marcia Tucker, the New Museum has grown into a respected and world-class institution. It was born out of Tucker's identification of a lack of critical engagement with the world of established ideas and traditions. Tucker had been a curator at the Whitney Museum and left when her commitment to the work of artists such as Richard Tuttle and Laurie Anderson became a source of controversy.

The first exhibition organised by the New Museum was held in 1978 at the New School. Five years later it moved to its current location on Broadway when Soho real estate was still as difficult to move as a piece of contemporary art by an unknown artist. The New Museum became tenant-owners, occupying the basement and ground floors, which were the only levels they could secure. The upper floors were left deserted, subject to break-ins, burst pipes and pigeon infestations, which the curatorial staff were left to deal with. The opportunity to expand properly to the higher floors only arose when the building was sold in 1996; the new owner agreed to swap the rear section of the ground floor area for the second floor.

Just before the expansion into the second floor, Dan Cameron was appointed as curator. Cameron had been an independent art critic and curator based in New York since 1979. He was familiar with the ethos of the institution, having curated a show at the old space in 1982. When Cameron became senior (and only!) curator his intention was to present

New Museum of Contemporary Art

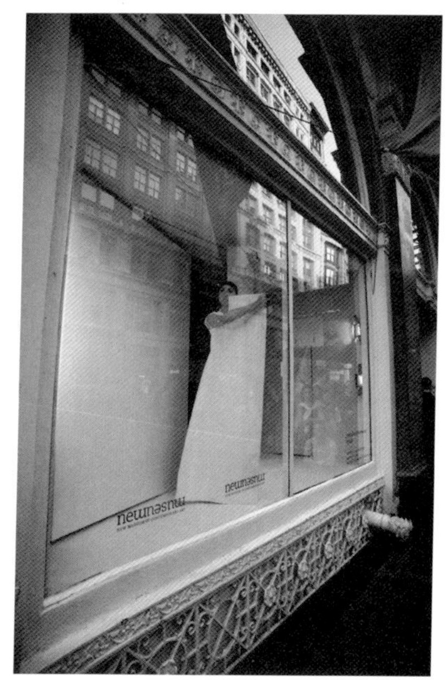

art in an aggressively historical format and to keep the New Museum in communication with like-minded institutions around the world. Cameron discussed with us how he perceived the aim of the New Museum:

Dan Cameron Our aim is to mobilise public recognition of art as a social force, reject elitism and over-specialisation of art. We believe that art is at the forefront of change in human consciousness and culture.

One of Cameron's long-term collaborators is Lisa Phillips, who was appointed director of the New Museum in April 1999. As curator of contemporary art at the Whitney Museum for more than 20 years, Phillips organised groundbreaking shows including *Beat Culture and the New America: 1950-65*, and presided over mid-career surveys of Richard Prince, Terry Winters and Cindy Sherman. Her curatorial vision has always been closely aligned with Dan Cameron's; thus, it will be exciting to witness what the duo concoct now they have the structure and resources of the museum to move their ideas forward.

The New Museum has an impressive track record for staging challenging and thought-provoking exhibitions. In 1994 Tucker organised the two-part exhibition *Bad Girls* which was conceived as a feminist carnival. Later that year the museum hosted another controversial exhibition. Performance artist Bob Flanagan installed himself in a hospital bed in the middle of the gallery space. The route to reaching him took the viewer through the challenges, difficulties, hopes and dreams of a man who was faced with terminal illness (cystic fibrosis) from the day he was born. The infamous video footage of Flanagan nailing his penis to a wooden board was definitely responsible for some of the controversy. In

New Museum of Contemporary Art

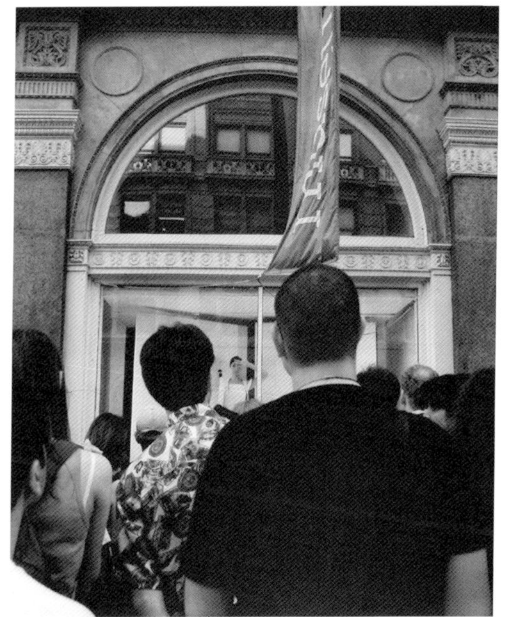

1999 *Fever: The Art of David Wojnarowicz* dealt with the similarly disturbing matter of AIDS.

With each exhibition a complementary education programme is hosted; this continues the museum's long-standing tradition in education. In fact, the New Museum was responsible for establishing the very first multi-cultural education programme, which became a model for others like it around the world.

As a publicly funded institution, the New Museum relies on several sources of income to complete its programme. Public money, foundations and private donations make up the bulk of their annual budget. The remainder is raised through its annual Gala Art Auction. It has become a privilege for contemporary artists to donate work in support of an institution that celebrates the extraordinary. Renowned as an important night on the art-world's social calendar, last year's was compered by none other than John Waters.

Part of the New Museum's expanded existence is a book store on the basement level. Cut from the floor plan of the ground level, the double height of the bookstore requires one to enter via a suspended staircase that connects the three-level atrium. More than 5000 volumes can be found on the shelves. The shop specialises in hard-to-find publications, exhibition catalogues and periodicals on contemporary art and culture from around the world, as well as unusual gifts and artists multiples (with prices starting as low as $150). Naturally, the bookshop carries the New Museum's publications, which have long been held in high esteem by academics and museum professionals. In addition to the books, an intriguing series of events are held in the bookshop. Readings and signings by popular authors, artists and critics have featured the likes of Marina Abramovic, Matthew Collings and Rosalind Krauss in the past year.

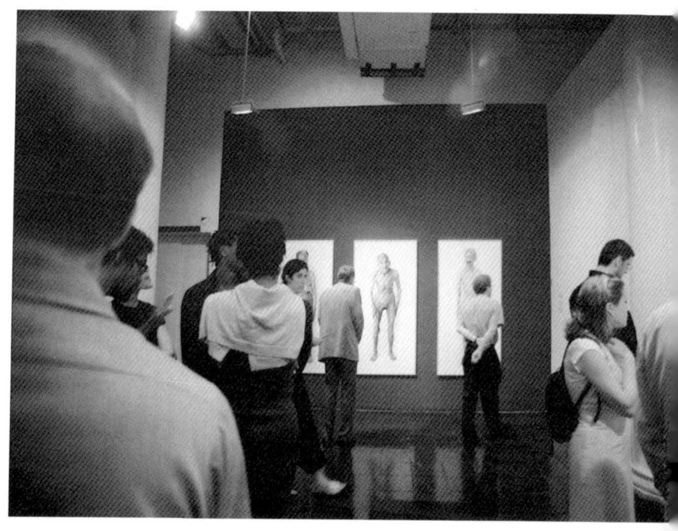

New Museum of Contemporary Art

The new millennium promises to continue embracing the New Museum's attitude to cutting-edge programming. *Picturing the Modern Amazon* sees three guest curators dealing with female images of hyper-muscular women, aka body builders. A mid-career retrospective of Tom Friedman as well as an exhibition of Rom Kazir's *Your Coloring Book* are also in the line-up.

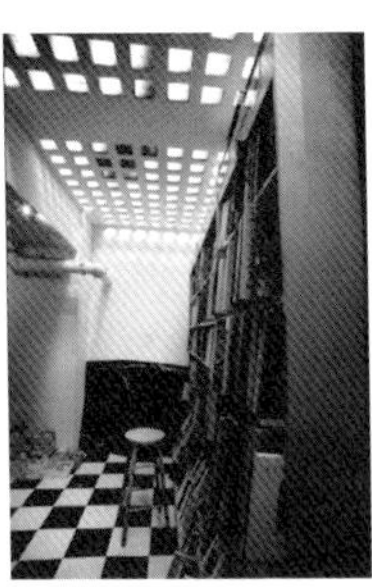

ADDRESS 583 Broadway, New York, NY10012
(212 219 1222)
WEBSITE www.newmu@newmuseum.org
OPEN Wednesday and Sunday, 12.00–18.00;
Thursday to Saturday, 12.00–20.00
SUBWAY Prince Street N, R

New Museum of Contemporary Art

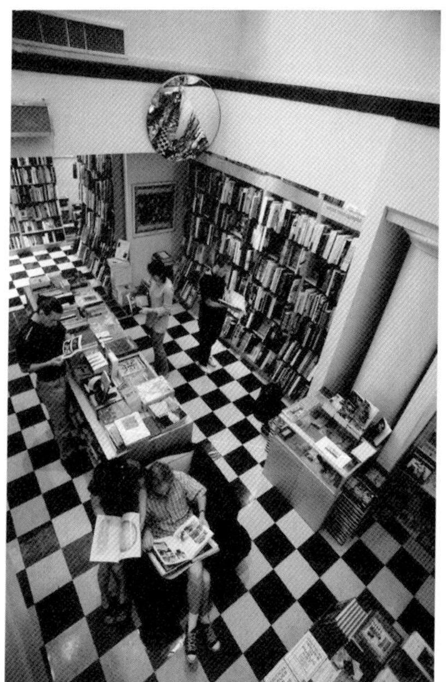

Scalo

Scalo publishes photographic books, often working with artists over several books. Nan Goldin has produced four books with Scalo, Robert Frank has six and Helmut Newton had his second out in 1999.

Scalo, based in Zurich, was founded in 1991 but the gallery space has only been open since October 1998 (the company already had an exhibition space in Zurich). The combination of office, gallery and bookstore is more than just an attractive resource. Associate publisher Theres Abbt, who runs the gallery, always intended it as a forum for contemporary art – books, prints and discussion. The primary show last autumn reflected this. 'The Pursuit of Justice' was a gallery talk given in conjunction with exhibitions from two Scalo books, *Deathly Still: Pictures of Concentration Camps* by Dirk Reinartz and *The Graves – Srebrenica and Vukovar* by Gilles Peres.

Scalo is located in yet another shopping-mall-for-galleries-style building. 560 Broadway is known for its photographic galleries. Julie Saul, Nancy Margolis and Ted Carter usually play host to the most interesting work. But Scalo's bookstore and commitment to utilising the space as a site of discourse make it the one to head for, even if it is only to browse through their delightful shelves where Issey Miyake rubs shoulders with John Waters and Larry Clark sits beside Karen Kilimnik. Scalo matches its name, the Italian for 'connecting point'.

ADDRESS Room 301, 560 Broadway, New York, NY 10012
(212 334 9393)
WEBSITE www.scalo.com
OPEN Monday to Saturday, 11.00–18.00
SUBWAY Prince Street N, R

Scalo

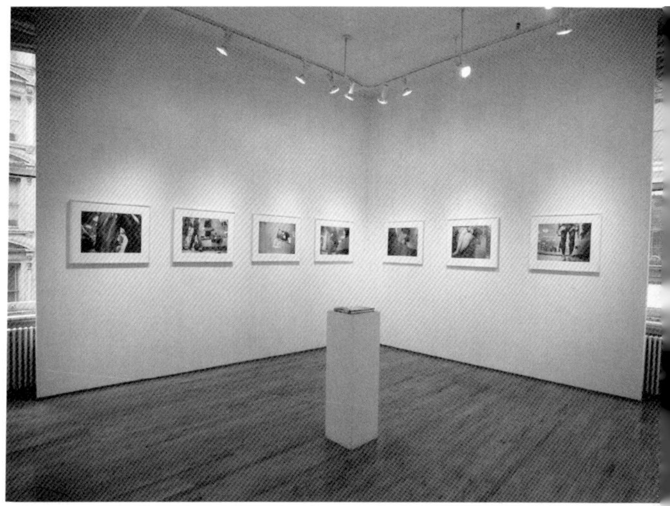

soho

Tony Shafrazi Gallery

2.58 Tony Shafrazi has been part of the contemporary art scene in New York for almost 30 years. Today, in its third incarnation, his gallery represents some of the work of leading artists from the past three decades including Andy Warhol, Patrick Demarchelier, Donald Baechler and Sandro Chia. During the 1980s Shafrazi was one of the hot-shot dealers of Soho, representing Jean-Michel Basquiat, Keith Haring and Kenny Scharf.

What Shafrazi may be most memorable for are his escapades as a young artist. In the early 1970s Shafrazi, who moved to New York from his native Iran in the 1960s, became part of the circle of conceptual artists that included Richard Serra and Robert Smithson. In 1974, Shafrazi committed an act that would go down in the annals of New York art history. After eight months of planning, Shafrazi smuggled a can of red spray paint into The Museum of Modern Art and proceeded to write 'Kill Lies All' on Picasso's 'Guernica'. Defacing a masterpiece of modern art was described by Shafrazi as a 'statement' rather than a political act. When the judge refused to accept traveller's cheques for payment of the $1000 bail, the artists gathered in the courtroom during his arraignment put forward the money. Not surprisingly, the incident garnered front-page news coverage throughout the world, which pleased Shafrazi. He correctly mused that art works at that time didn't often make headlines. Although he was never arrested for the act, Shafrazi immediately became a notorious figure, supported by many of the artists of his generation, although particularly despised by the curator of modern art at the MOMA.

The most recent scandal that Shafrazi has been involved with involves the great British artist Francis Bacon. After Bacon's death, there was controversy over who would be in charge of the estate of the artist. Bacon's lover, who was heir to the estate, insisted that Shafrazi look after it, rather than the Marlborough Gallery, which had represented the artist

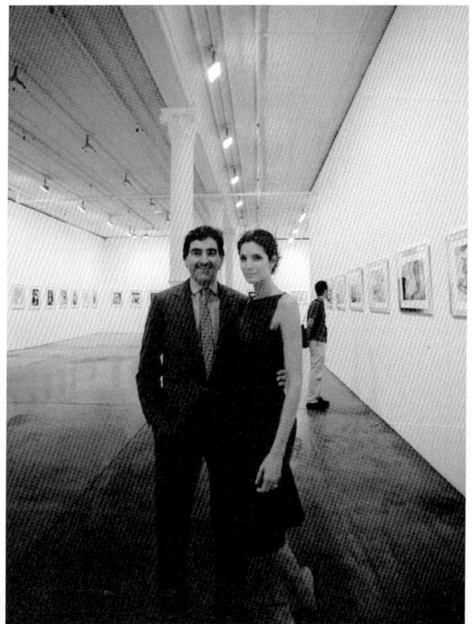

for many years. As the sole proprietor of Bacon's work, which now commands prices in the millions and is internationally revered, Shafrazi's financial security is set in stone.

Shafrazi's chutzpah may precede him, yet it has proved to be his best asset.

ADDRESS 119 Wooster Street, New York, NY 10012 (212 274 9300)
OPEN Tuesday to Saturday, 10.00–18.00
SUBWAY Canal Street A, C, E

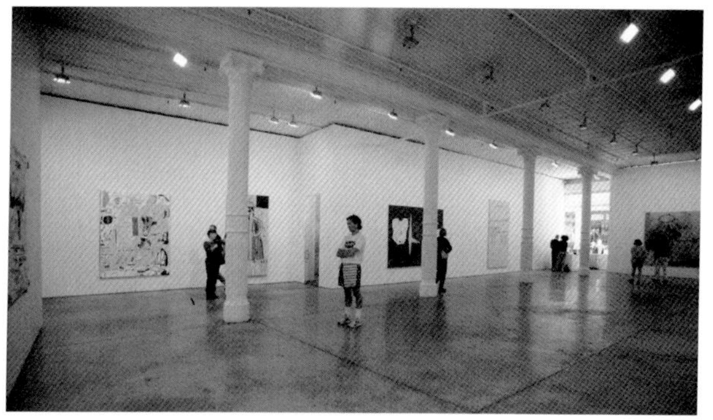

Holly Solomon Gallery

2.62 Holly Solomon is a legend in the New York art world. One of the leading figures in contemporary art dealing, Solomon has survived for more than two decades. Through the turbulent times of the 1980s and the more conservative decade of the 1990s, she has remained a steadfast part of the scene.

Solomon is interested in virtually every type of art form, from multiples and drawings to performance and installation. She represents American and European artists, especially those related to the Fluxus movement, pop and minimal art, all of which Solomon was witness to in her many years of dealing.

Although Solomon can be relied upon for secondary market staples such as Sonia Delaunay, Gordon-Matta Clark, Andy Warhol and Joan Mitchell, she has recently concentrated on showing the work of less well-known artists. In the last two years she has hosted solo shows by Mengbo Feng, Nick Waplington, and Pier Luigi Consagra. However, she has also mounted works by Nam June Paik and William Wegman.

This huge space may not show the cutting-edge work that Solomon once pioneered, but her perseverance and staying power earn this gallerist a place in Manhattan's art-world archives.

ADDRESS 172 Mercer Street, New York, NY 10012 (212 941 5777)
OPEN Tuesday to Saturday, 10.00–18.00
SUBWAY Houston B, D, F, Q/Prince Street N, R

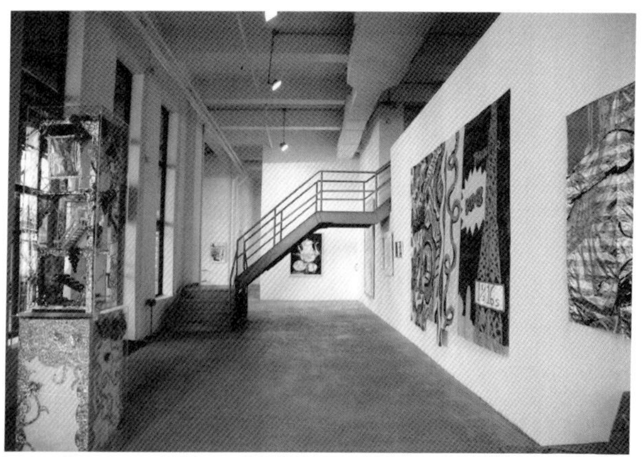

Sperone Westwater

David Sperone and Angela Westwater have built an empire. They represent a host of the biggest names in the business, and are based in two white-cube rooms in Soho.

Perhaps their most interesting artist is Bruce Nauman. This recluse – who sometimes doesn't even speak on the telephone to curators of his exhibitions, let alone meet them in person – has produced one of the most impressive bodies of work this century. His work consists mainly of videos that derive from performances made in his studio. Nauman has brought body art to a new level and, like Duchamp, he changed the viewer's relationship to the work of art. A Nauman piece demands participation, especially his neon text pieces which necessarily implicate the viewer who reads them.

Sperone Westwater also represent Nauman's wife, Susan Rothenberg, a highly regarded painter. Rothenberg and Nauman live a secluded life on a ranch in New Mexico. Richard Tuttle – one of Nauman and Rothenberg's New Mexican neighbours – is also represented by Sperone Westwater. Tuttle has made a career out of using ordinary materials; in his work MDF, Styrofoam, and string are transformed into transcendental pieces of sculpture.

The gallery's list of artists continues in a who's who of creativity: Alighiero E Boetti, Francesco Clemente, Peter Halley, Guillermo Kuitca, Wolfgang Laib, Mario Merz, Mimmo Paladino, Michelangelo Pistoletto, Gerhard Richter, and Cy Twombly are all shown at Sperone Westwater.

ADDRESS 142 and 121 Greene Street, New York, NY 10012 (212 431 3685)
OPEN Tuesday to Saturday, 10.00–18.00
SUBWAY Prince Street N, R

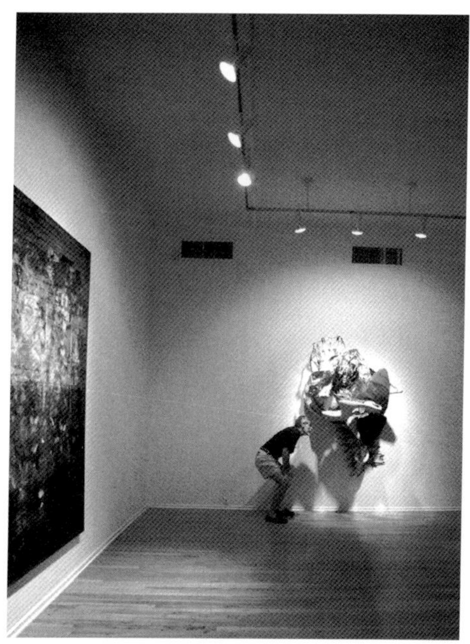

SI/NY (Swiss Institute New York)

Unexpected eccentricities may be found on the third floor of this sober downtown building. Departing from the classic image of its homeland, the Swiss Institute offers an alternative view of Swiss culture. This contemporary approach is reflected in the architecture of the loft and the wacky exhibition displays, talks by distinguished artists and curators, screenings, performance art and live music that make up its season of events.

Set up in 1986 as an independent non-profit organisation, the Institute aims to promote artistic dialogue between Switzerland and the United States. Exploring contemporary and historical avenues, it emphasises the unique qualities of Switzerland's cultural heritage and its place in the context of America. What sounds like a very dry mission is actually delivered to the public through an intriguing and refreshing programme that covers many disciplines.

Only the open-minded should enter the space as much of the Institute's programming is designed to give a platform to 'experimental art' – a phrase that could at times also be a synonym for inferior art. However, much of the work presented is top quality, including the exhibition of Roman Signer's work that was staged in 1997. The performance, 'I Was Here', that opened the show included Signer, in his trademark black rubber boots, stepping on to an ink pad and then raising himself on a rope to the ceiling, where he made a set of footprints. A tongue-in-cheek reference to the brief amount of time spent in the gallery by most visitors, the remains of the performance – the rope, boots and prints – were left in the gallery as a sculpture.

Another noteworthy exhibition was held in 1998. *Profession Obsession: The Daniel Spoerri Archives* presented a selection from the archives that the artist donated to The Swiss National Library in 1966. As a

SI/NY (Swiss Institute New York)

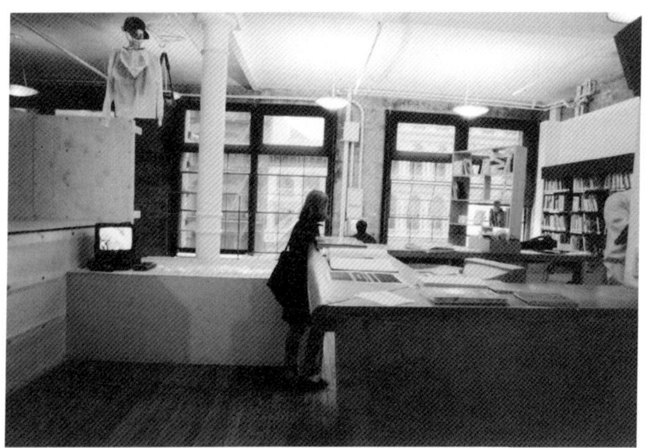

founding member of Le Nouveau Realisme and Fluxus, Spoerri occupies a centrally important but much overlooked role in the development of contemporary conceptual art.

An important element of the Swiss Institute is its library, which focuses on contemporary visual and performing arts. This features approximately 3000 volumes including Swiss periodicals, exhibition catalogues, CD-ROMs, books and videos, and is presided over by the new library curator Susanne Reichling. An invaluable resource for students and other researchers, the library is in plain view of the gallery visitor and occupies a prime location in the loft. Some of that Swiss pragmatism is seeping through after all.

ADDRESS 3rd floor, 495 Broadway, New York, NY 10012 (212 925 2035)
WEBSITE www.swissinstitute.net
OPEN Tuesday to Saturday, 11.00–18.00
SUBWAY Prince Street N, R

SI/NY (Swiss Institute New York)

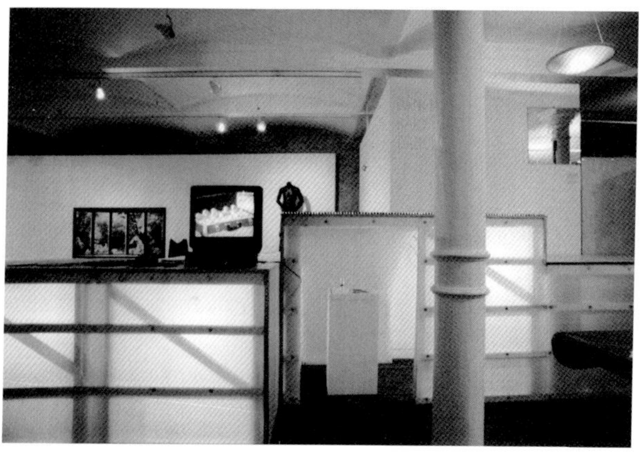

Thread Waxing Space

Thread Waxing Space's mission statement explains that a major aim is to exhibit emerging artists. This may be confusing to those who witnessed the 1999 group show *Conceptual Art as Neurological Praxis*, featuring work by the well-established likes of Douglas Gordon, Liam Gillick and Jack Pierson. The abundance of work proved to detract from the pieces themselves; while Thread Waxing Space boasts 7500 square feet of space, curator Warren Neidich filled it to bursting.

Originally created to explore issues in abstract painting, the vast dimensions of the gallery have led artists of all media to bring experimental work to fruition here. Only established in 1991, Thread Waxing Space is a non-profit organisation incorporated under the University of the State of New York as an education facility. It was founded by Timothy U Nye and its aim is to present inter-disciplinary events (exhibitions, performances, musical concerts, readings, panel discussions) by and with artists early in their careers. Like other institutions of this type, Thread Waxing Space is keen to make contemporary projects more accessible to the public. Part of this commitment is an education programme that services the immediate area as well as the five boroughs of New York.

While Thread Waxing Space has the funding to commission work, and bring together 'high' and 'low' art under one roof in some very effective group shows, the fact remains that it is awkwardly located on the second floor of commercial Broadway. In addition the long narrow space is not conducive to showing work as effectively as possible. That said; you never know what you'll see, so check it out regardless.

ADDRESS 476 Broadway, New York, NY 10013 (212 966 9520)
OPEN Tuesday to Saturday, 10.00–18.00
SUBWAY Canal Street 1, 9

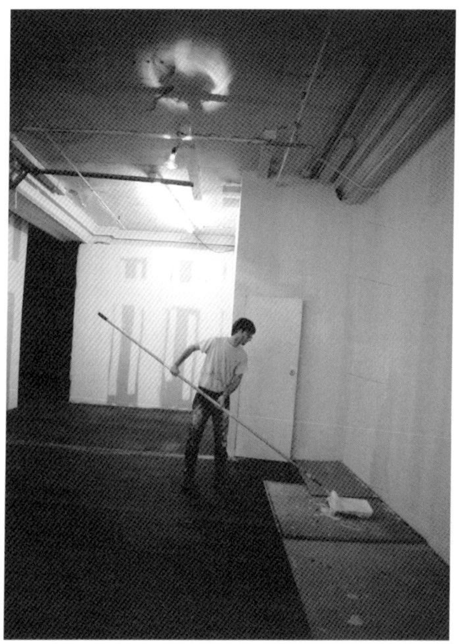

Jack Tilton

Jack Tilton is something of an anomaly among Soho dealers. Although he has been in the business for years, Tilton remains positively grounded and untainted by the chaos of the art world that surrounds him. His first job in New York was at the former Betty Parsons Gallery on West 57th Street. Famous for showing the very fashionable abstract expressionists, Parsons was an excellent mentor from whom to learn the ropes of dealing.

In 1991 Tilton set up his own gallery on Greene Street. He represents about 15 artists at any one time and has shown the work of many early in their careers. (For example, Tilton gave Douglas Gordon his first show in New York and had the foresight to show Zhang Pelli before he became fashionable.) Most are emerging artists, many of whom are from China and the Far East. Tilton finds the discourse of the post-Tianemen Square generation stimulating and fondly recounts the experience of meeting artists at the Art Bar in Beijing. It says something about Tilton's eye for talent that many of the young Chinese artists that he had previously shown, such as Wei Dong, appeared in the 1999 Venice Biennale.

Exhibitions range from solo and group presentations (two or three times a year) to curated shows. Tilton encourages gallery staff to curate at least one show a year, a result of the frustration he suffered at Betty Parsons Gallery where such group efforts never took place.

Tilton is also involved with some secondary dealing, something for which he is less well known; this kind of business provides him with the necessary capital to support interesting projects by young artists.

ADDRESS 49 Greene Street, New York, NY 10013 (212 941 1775/ JTILTONG@earthlink.net)
OPEN Tuesday to Saturday, 10.00–18.00
SUBWAY Spring Street C, E

Jack Tilton

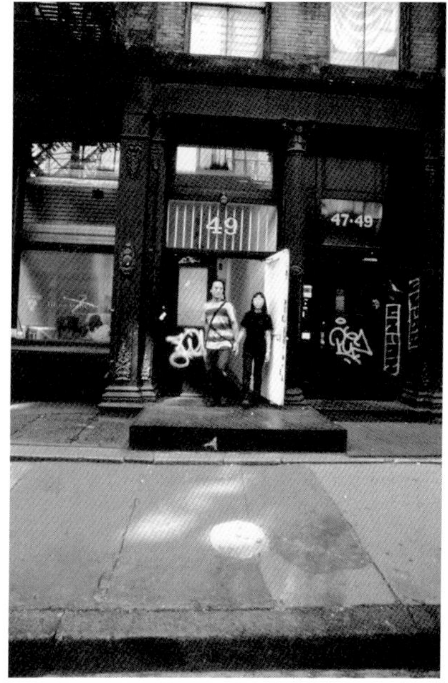

Visionaire Gallery

To any member of the international trendygentsia, the word 'visionaire' conjures up a magical image. This publication produced its first issue in spring 1991. It aims to offer a forum for themed work by both famous and emerging artists as well as celebrities, fashion designers, art directors and image makers. The manifesto has lured the likes of Richard Avedon, Bruce Weber, Helmut Newton, Karl Lagerfeld, Cindy Sherman, Helmut Lang, Barbara Kruger and John Galliano to create, curate or provide work for this multi-format album.

Visionaire was created by Stephen Gan, Cecelia Dean and James Kaliardos. When they moved their offices to Mercer Street the possibility of another forum in which to present work came up – and the Visionaire Gallery was born. Programmed by the team, it features curated shows and reflects the life and inspirations of *Visionaire*. Solo shows by Testino and Meisel are high on the agenda, as are *Visionaire* retrospectives.

Visionaire (the album) is published three or four times a year. Each issue is produced as a limited edition. Issue 24, guest edited by Tom Ford for Gucci, came as a lightbox and featured work that Peter Saville, Alexander McQueen, Mario Testino, Nick Knight, Wolfgang Tillmans and Ines Van Lambsweerde created for this format. The Fantasy Issue (26) was 72 pages of round prints or round objects supplied by Todd Haynes, David Byrne, Tony Oursler, Christian Lacroix, Isaac Mizrahi and Manolo Blahnik.

A visit to the gallery is the next best thing to actually owning a copy of your favourite issue of *Visionaire*.

ADDRESS 11 Mercer Street, New York, NY 10013 (212 274 8959)
WEBSITE www.visionaireworld.com
OPEN Monday to Friday, 12.00–18.00; Saturday, 13.00–18.00
SUBWAY Canal Street N, R

Visionaire Gallery

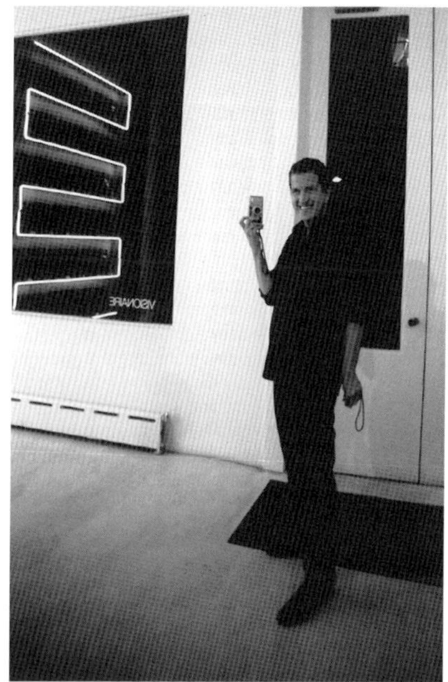

Water Tower

Water Tower is a work made in the 'traditional' vein of public art; meaning to be placed outside in an urban setting. An artist best known for her notorious sculpture 'House', a cast of the inside of an entire London house, Rachel Whiteread was the perfect choice for a public-art commission in New York City. Public Art Fund, a non-profit visual-arts organisation that commissions and presents temporary exhibitions throughout New York City, joined forces with the Beck's art sponsorship programme to produce a monumental piece of art. Public Art Fund occupies a unique position within the art world because it exists outside the traditional context of museums and galleries. It brings contemporary art into the public sphere and exposes diverse audiences to art in unexpected places. An axample is Barbara Krugers' 'Bus'. This is a NYC bus, covered with Kruger's signature bold text and simple imagery, which carries passengers from Midtown Manhattan to Queens. Public Art Fund attempts to forge lasting relationships between artists, communities, and the city.

'Water Tower', Whiteread's project, is her first public sculpture in the US and the result of more than four years of planning and negotiating. Whiteread travelled to New York several times to research sites and locations throughout the city. She became fascinated with the idea of maintaining a presence within the urban environment without imposing a physical intrusion on a community in which the artist did not live. The flux, noise, and movement of the city cautioned the artist against locations most commonly associated with public sculpture. While walking under the Brooklyn side of the Manhattan Bridge, Whiteread noticed the skyline dotted with wooden water towers. Thus the vernacular architecture suggested a possible exploration of the significance of anonymous architecture as sculptural form.

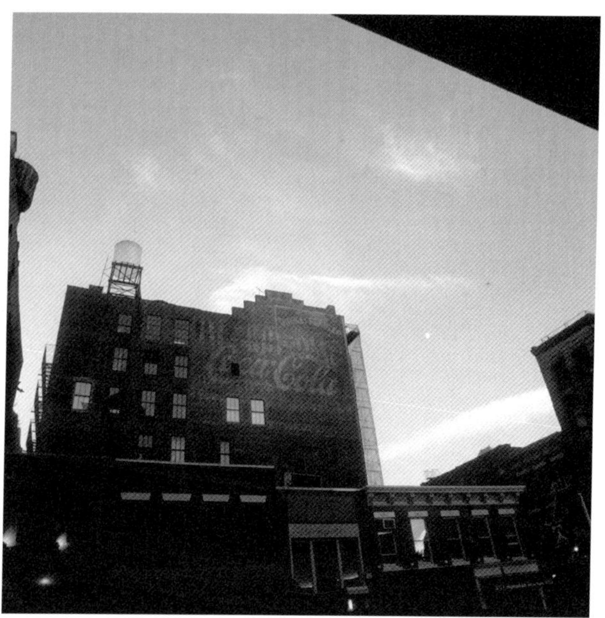
Coca-Cola

Water Tower

During spring 1998 Whiteread lived in New York where she made drawings, plans and models of the project. A wooden tank was carefully removed from the rooftop of an Upper East Side building and reconstructed in a studio in Chelsea. Whiteread worked with a fabricator to determine the best method for casting. The tank served as a mould for a resin cast which took four months to complete. Once the mould was removed a monolithic form with 3-inch-thick walls was revealed. It is a translucent resin cast of the interior of a once-functioning water tower. In June 1998 the 8-ton sculpture was hoisted to the roof of a Soho apartment (if you want to see it up close you must make arrangements to walk through the apartment that it rests on) and became visible from street level at the corner of West Broadway and Grand Street.

'Water Tower' represents various things. Tangibly it is the largest project ever to be commissioned by the Public Art Fund. On an ideological level it stands for contemporary art successfully installed in an urban environment. It is also emblematic of the intricate relationship between public art and architecture. It proves that as far as public sculpture is concerned the two disciplines are categorically and necessarily intertwined.

ADDRESS corner of West Broadway and Grand Street, New York, (212 980 4575)
WEBSITE www.publicartfund.org
SUBWAY Canal Street A, C, E

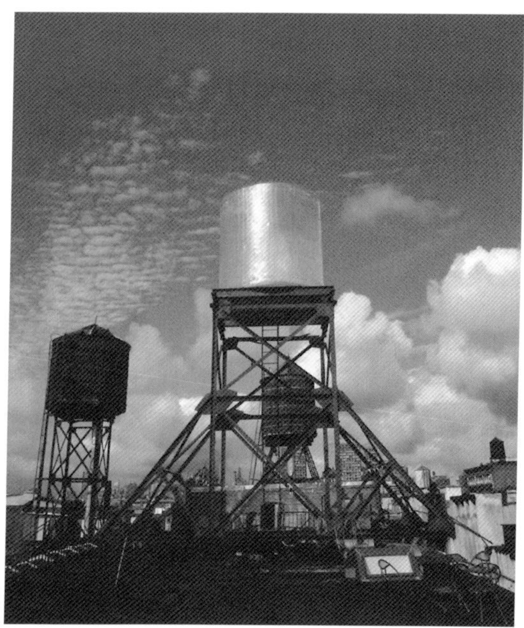

David Zwirner

2.80 The name Zwirner is associated with galleries in both Cologne and New York. David Zwirner grew up in a family of dealers in his native Germany. He arrived in New York 15 years ago and played jazz in a band alongside working for the Brooke Alexander Gallery. In 1993 he was finally ready to open up on his own and found the attractive and spacious site on Greene Street that now houses the David Zwirner Gallery.

Representing artists such as Stan Douglas and Diana Thater, Zwirner was committed to film and video as a method of expression long before it became fashionable and commonplace, and loves artists who work with moving imagery.

His other ten artists work on paper, in sculpture – which is another personal love – and with installation. It is a testimony to his uniquely shaped space with distinctively high ceilings that he can effectively show such a variety of works.

Zwirner's flock maintains a high profile and is consistently shown elsewhere; American artist Ray Pettibon recently had a solo exhibition in The Drawing Center and Stan Douglas was shown alongside Douglas Gordon at the Dia Center for the Arts. More importantly, their names regularly appear at the Venice and Whitney Biennales.

Zwirner also represent the estate of Gordon Matta-Clark and handles and exhibits works by contemporary masters such as Joseph Beuys, Dan Flavin, On Kawara and Bruce Nauman.

ADDRESS 43 Greene Street, New York, NY 10013 (212 966 9074)
WEBSITE www.davidzwirner.com
OPEN Tuesday to Saturday, 10.00–18.00
SUBWAY Spring Street C, E

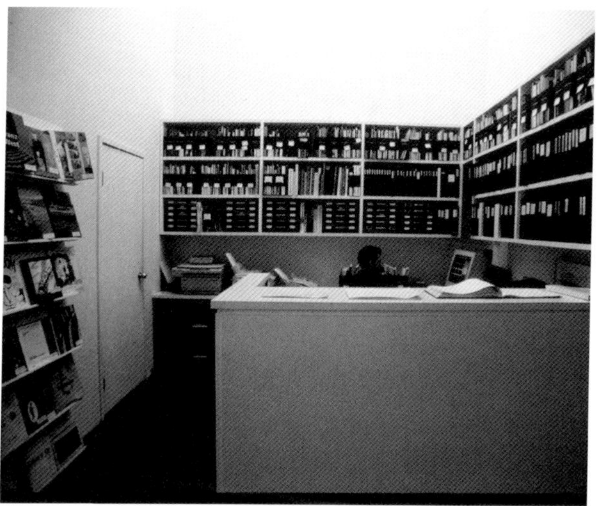

lower west side

The New School University Collection 3.2

The New School University Collection

The New School for Social Research is not so new. It was founded in 1919, when two professors from the uptown Columbia University got into a dispute over freedom of expression; they decided that they needed a more liberal platform from which to discuss contemporary society. In 1929 The New School moved to its current home (although it is now spread over three main sites) in the first international-style building in New York, designed by the Vienna Secessionist architect Joseph Urban. The excitement the building generated led both Jose Clemente Orozco and Thomas Hart Benton to create murals for it. Considered treasures and still on display, they make up part of a 1100-strong collection of art.

The New School expanded its international base with the establishment of the University of Exile in 1933. This provided a haven for intellectuals and artists escaping totalitarian regimes in Europe. Later changing its name to the Graduate Faculty, notable figures such as Meyer Schapiro, George Grosz, John Cage, Larry Rivers and Ronald Bladen taught there. Martha Graham and Aaron Copland collaborated with Isamu Noguchi to create *Appalachian Spring* at the New Museum.

In the mid 1980s, the decision was made to hire a curator. Enter Kathleen Goncharov, a museum-trained curator who is responsible for the New School's contemporary art acquisitions. Because the New School does not see its role as a museum, it has developed a policy of selling on art when it becomes too valuable. With the money generated, Goncharov is able to buy new work.

The collection is displayed throughout the lobbies, halls and conference rooms of The New School (there has been no gallery here since the 1950s). At the moment the work of Lorna Simpson, Roxy Paine, Joseph Beuys, Nancy Spero and Willie Dogherty can be seen on long-term display. Walking through the buildings, visitors encounter work by Cindy

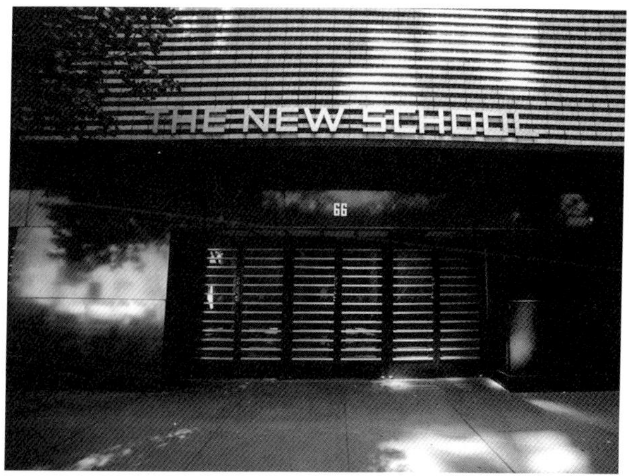
THE NEW SCHOOL
66

Sherman, Mariko Mori, Ann Hamilton, Tracey Moffatt, Adrian Piper, Thomas Struth, Kiki Smith, Kara Walker and David Hammons.

A bridge connecting two wings of the main building overlooks a courtyard open to the public in-the-know. Martin Puryear and architect Michael Van Valkenburgh collaborated with the aim of producing an environment that would function as a site for both relaxation and special outdoor events. Each level of the bridge is used to display art or mini-exhibitions curated by faculty and/or students.

The bulk of the collection has been acquired through donations from artists, collectors and dealers. However the 'revolving collection' (as Goncharov has identified the policy of purchasing new art with money made from selling older, more valuable pieces) is supplemented with funds from Vera List. This philanthropist donates both work and capital to the New School. Her generous support has helped the collection grow into the progressively reflective body it is today.

The New School's collection is still only seen by students and staff. In fact, anyone can have access to the buildings simply by asking the security men on the door. Yet perhaps this is for the best. Goncharov has emphasised that the School does not have the security measures required to protect the work. Since her appointment, works by Andreas Gursky and Sue Coe have sadly gone missing. It is unfortunate in this case that the public has taken advantage of an institution that was effectively – and uniquely – set up for their pleasure and education.

ADDRESS 66 West 12th Street, New York, NY 10011 (212 229 5667)
WEBSITE www.newschool.edu
HOURS weekdays, term-time (subject to school hours)
SUBWAY 14th Street 1, 2, 3, 9, F, L

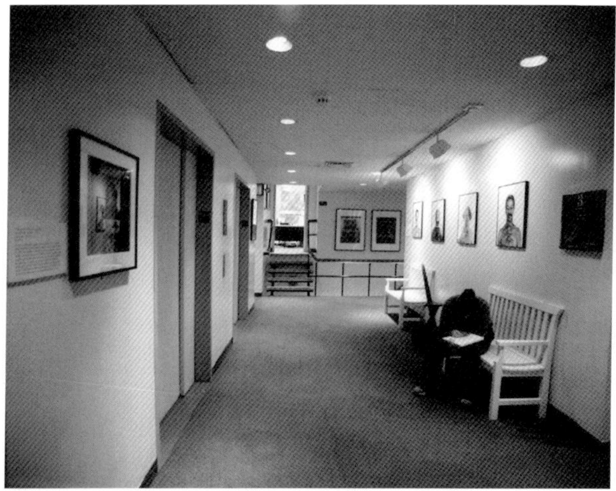

chelsea

529 West 20th Street

Also known as Chelsea's tribute to a shopping mall of galleries, 529 is an 11-storey building that houses an astounding 19 galleries (each floor averages two or three).

A stroll through the space (we strongly recommend that visitors take the elevator to the top floor and work their way down), will certainly provide a wide range of eye candy. Yet it is inevitable that with such a high density of galleries (let alone the fact that there are more than two other spaces on the same block), you are going to see a large amount of very poor work.

529 is the disappointing result of the mass exodus of Soho galleries into Chelsea, and the gallery dealers' fierce competition for the best sites. Although some of the galleries in the building have plenty of space and great light, there is no getting away from the feeling that you are passing through a vast number of white cubes.

That is not to say that there aren't some treasures to be found within this chest. Our favourite is Derek Eller who has an eye for talent and shows a variety of young and hip artists including the painter Jovi Schnell. Andrew Kreps, Margaret Thatcher Projects and I-20 are also worth a visit.

ADDRESS 529 West 20th Street, New York, NY 10011
TELEPHONE see individual galleries in *Gallery Guide*
TRANSPORT 23rd Street C, E

529 West 20th Street

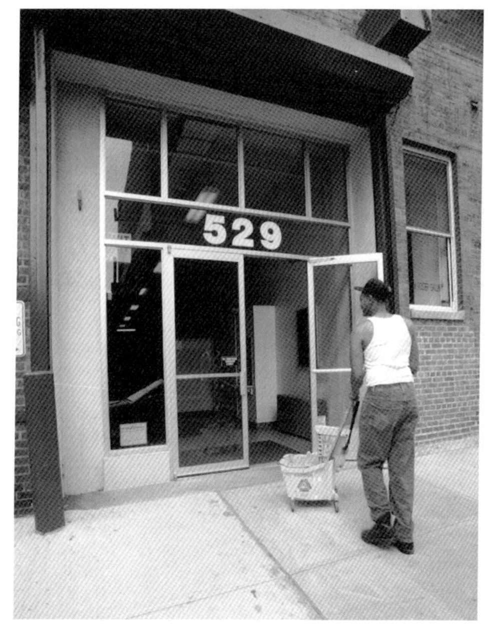

Gavin Brown's Enterprise, Corp.

4.4 Representing the likes of Billy Name, Chris Ofili, Elizabeth Peyton, and Steven Pippin, one wouldn't expect Gavin Brown to have started his gallery on a shoestring. In fact, Brown began with only $17,000 from sympathetic collectors and nothing in the bank.

A Londoner, Brown landed in New York to participate in the Whitney Museum's prestigious Independent Study Programme as an artist. Through a job on the desk at Gallery 303 he came into contact with art-world wheelers and dealers and, while still at 303, Brown began to represent the then less-well-known artist Steven Pippin (subsequently short-listed for the 1999 Turner Prize). After New York's Museum of Modern Art bought a sculpture by Pippin, Brown knew that he had to open his own space or risk losing the artist. And thus was his enterprise born.

On the fringes of Chelsea, Brown's enterprise is much less glamorous than its neighbours. A dusty orange storefront without a name serves as the portal to the space. The gallery is set back from the street and now features an adjacent bar with a *Saturday Night Live* discotheque-style floor.

Brown has always been unusual in his approach. He has curated a show in an office and is equally likely to show work in the new bar. His attitude draws inspiration from the many artist-run spaces of his native country. But Gavin Brown's Enterprise, Corp. is a commercial venture operating in a commercial world, and Gavin is keen to sell work. And, if you're not interested in any of it, he can always sell you a beer.

ADDRESS 436 West 15th Street, New York, NY 10013 (212 627 5258/ bar 212 206 7321/passerby@bway.net)
OPEN Tuesday to Saturday 10.00–18.00/bar Tuesday to Saturday 18.00–late
SUBWAY 14th Street A, C, E, L

Gavin Brown's Enterprise, Corp.

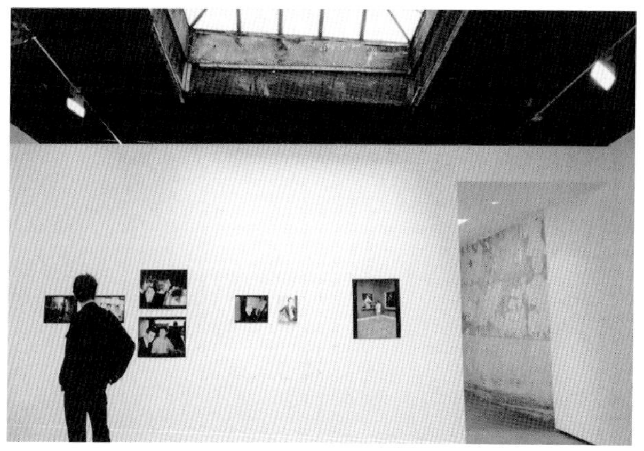

Paula Cooper Gallery

Even people without an interest in contemporary art should visit the Paula Cooper Gallery. The sheer size and atmosphere of the award-winning space make it memorable. Natural light filtered through a cathedral ceiling, complete with vast wooden rafters, gives the gallery, which occupies a 19th-century building, an almost ethereal character. When Brian O'Doherty wrote about the white space of the gallery as a quasi-religious experience in his essay 'Inside the White Cube', he must have had this type of place in mind.

But Cooper has a formidable audience to impress. In addition to her peers in the art world, she deals with the highest echelon of collectors of contemporary art. The artistic agenda of Cooper focuses almost entirely on conceptual and minimalist work – now quite lucrative genres. The gallery shows work by Carl Andre, Dan Flavin, Donald Judd, Yayoi Kusama, Sol Lewitt and Joel Shapiro. The clean lines and simple forms of Judd and Andre have been emulated by furniture designers and architects, and meet the ethos of the gallery.

Some of these artists have been working with Cooper since the gallery was founded in 1968; for example Sol LeWitt first exhibited a wall drawing at Paula Cooper Gallery in 1968. Cooper's was the first art gallery to open in New York's Soho district, and obviously she helped create a geographical shift that would last for two decades. She remained steadfast in Soho until 1996, when she was among the first to start the exodus to Chelsea.

By sporadically mounting some exhibitions of historical importance, Cooper has not been afraid to court controversy. Robert Gober, who makes art based on his own identity as a homosexual raised as a Catholic, presented pivotal work on gender and identity in 1989. More recently Gober has outraged the Vatican by exhibiting a statue of the Virgin Mary

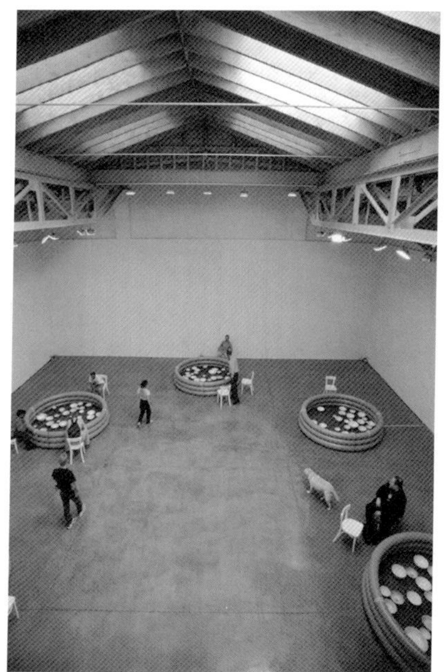

with a lead pipe impaling her torso. Cooper also shows Andres Serrano, the photographer notorious for his 'Piss Christ' photographs. Using a wide array of props and settings, Serrano has depicted such unlikely subjects as corpses in a morgue, Ku Klux Klan members and the sex lives of (among others) dwarfs and hermaphrodites.

The Paula Cooper Gallery is also well known for hosting concerts, benefits and lectures including marathon readings of works by James Joyce and Gertrude Stein that have the added appeal of having been held annually on New Year's Eve for the past 20 years.

ADDRESS 534 West 21st Street, New York, NY 10011 (212 255 1105)
OPEN Tuesday to Saturday, 10.00–18.00
SUBWAY 23rd Street C, E

Paula Cooper Gallery

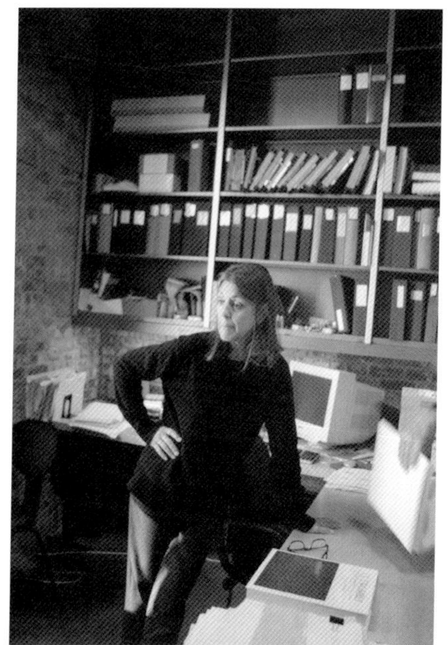

DIA Center for the Arts

May all contemporary art lovers pay homage to this, their inspiration, aspiration and perhaps even mentor. The Dia Center for the Arts has not unjustly been called the god of contemporary galleries and is generally highly regarded by patrons of art the world over.

The name Dia, taken from the Greek word meaning 'through', suggests the Center's role in enabling extraordinary artistic projects to be realised. For the past 20 years , the Dia Center for the Arts has played a vital and original role among arts institutions both in America and the rest of the world by initiating, supporting, presenting and preserving projects in nearly every artistic medium and creating a locus for interdisciplinary art and criticism.

In the 1970s Dia supported long-term projects that could not be accommodated in museums or conventional galleries because of their nature or scale. At the height of the land art movement (artists objecting to their work being presented in gallery spaces that would confine and commodify it) Dia commissioned Walter De Maria's 'The Lightning Field', 'The Broken Kilometer' (see page 2.14), and 'The New York Earth Room' (see page 2.22) all within the space of two years.

Unlike the other two installations, 'The Lightning Field' is not located in New York, but in the desolate desert of southwestern New Mexico. De Maria chose the site because of its isolation and the lightning storms that proliferate in the area during the summer. Visitors must book in advance as they are driven by four-wheel-drive vehicle out to a cabin on the edge of the site. A field containing 400 stainless-steel poles that attract the lightning is all that is on view from the cabin where visitors must spend the night. The spectacle is provided by lightning storms, which of course the Dia cannot guarantee. Not only does experiencing 'The Lightning Field' allow visitors to commune with art in nature at its most raw, but

DIA Center for the Arts

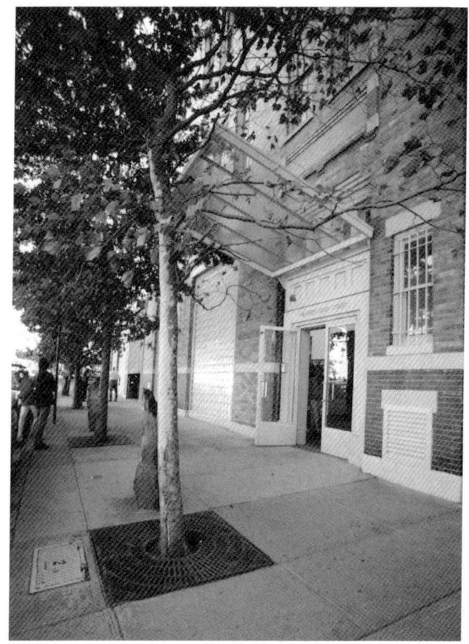

you never know who you will wind up bunking with; the cabin only sleeps six!

Another ambitious (in both size and location) project that Dia supported was Donald Judd's dream of creating an alternative exhibition space in the desert town of Marfa, Texas, just 60 miles north of the Mexican border. For Judd, the ideal environment for viewing minimalist sculpture was outside of the museum, which constricted works because of lack of space. In Marfa, Dia purchased four disused artillery sheds which Judd went on to inhabit with his work and that of his colleagues. There are also 15 large concrete sculptures scattered through the landscape adjacent to the sheds. Eventually Judd went on to acquire more buildings in Marfa (much to the bemusement and alarm of the locals). Unfortunately, Judd fell out with Dia when his demands became excessive. After a lengthy legal battle the buildings and artwork purchased with the help of Dia were left in Judd's care. This part of the project is now called The Chinati Foundation, named after the local mountain range. Everything (art and buildings) bought with Judd's personal funds is now termed The Donald Judd Foundation.

Not all of Dia's support has been so unappreciated. The institution has also commissioned Dan Flavin's installation at Bridgehampton, New York, where nine of his works have been on view in a renovated firehouse since 1983. In the decade from 1974 to 1984 Dia collected many of the works by a focused group of artists. These activities were initially funded by Philippa de Menil and Heiner Friedrich. Amassing a collection that is representative of pop, minimalism, conceptual and earth works, Dia bought Joseph Beuys, John Chamberlain, Imi Knoebel, Blinky Palermo, Cy Twombly, Fred Sandback and Andy Warhol.

It was only in 1987 that Dia opened a large exhibition facility in a

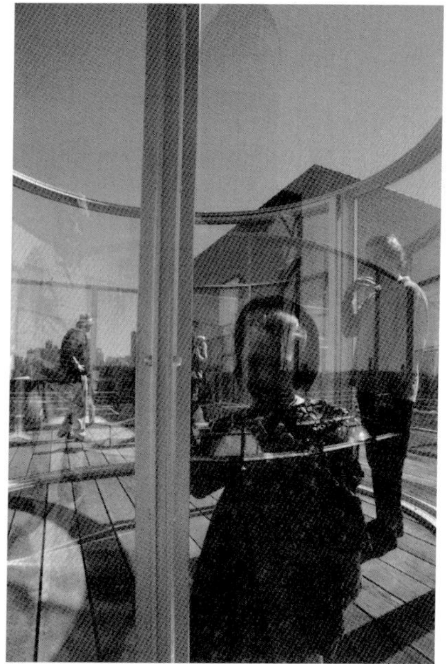

40,000-square-foot former warehouse renovated by Richard Gluckman. Besides the Kitchen, they were the only institution to exhibit art in what was at the time an industrial wasteland. They dedicate this space, and another they acquired across the street, to large-scale long-term (approximately six months) exhibitions. It is a Dia tradition that all the artists who participate in the site-specific projects meet the institution's mission statement, which is to make the arts of today accessible to a wide and well-informed audience. Jenny Holzer, Tim Rollins and the Kids of Survival (K.O.S.), Lawrence Weiner, Dan Graham, Brice Marden, On Kawara, Ann Hamilton and Alighiero e Boetti have all created projects especially for Dia. More recently Jessica Stockholder, Robert Irwin, Stan Douglas and Douglas Gordon have produced visionary and insightful pieces.

On top of their main building in 1991 Dia commissioned seminal artist Dan Graham to create a permanent installation. Drawing on his passion for architecture, art and music, Graham created a piece that encompasses all three. 'The Urban Rooftop Project' is a pavilion constructed of two-way mirrored glass, which shifts between transparent and reflective states as the intensity of light changes. This creates a dizzying effect for the viewer, who becomes part of the piece, standing inside a cylinder, which is in turn inside a square. The dramatic skyline is reflected on and by the glass walls. Adjacent to the pavilion, Graham transformed a former utility shed to a coffee bar that features a video programme selected by the artist.

The basalt stone columns that line 22nd Street are also part of Dia's artistic programme. They form the continuation of a project begun at *Documenta 7* in 1982 by Joseph Beuys, which called for the planting of 7000 trees paired with basalt stones throughout the city of Kassel. Dia helped Beuys with the project, which was completed five years later with

DIA Center for the Arts

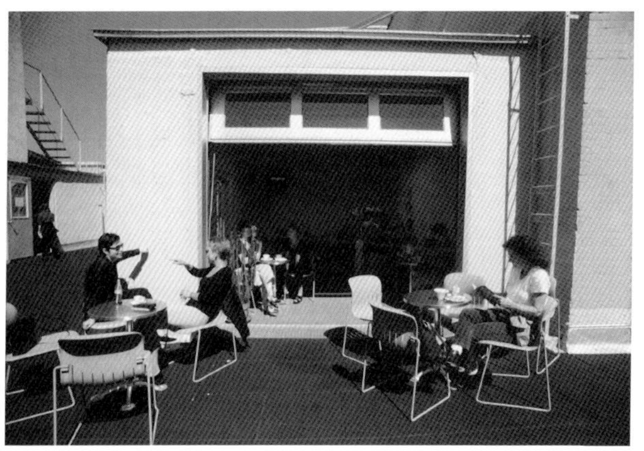

the planting of the last tree at *Documenta 8* in 1987. The trees and stone columns on 22nd Street mark Dia's commitment to Beuys's plan to extend the project all over world.

Besides the long-term projects, Dia is also home to a highly regarded events programme that includes the Robert Lehman Lectures on Contemporary Art and a series called Readings in Contemporary Poetry. Michael Govan, director, and Lynn Cooke, Dia's impressive curator, manage to strike a balance between the intellectual and the dynamic at the Dia. Their impressive website, which has been nominated for awards, attests to the varied and innovative vision of Dia's team.

ADDRESS 548 West 22nd Street, New York, NY 10011 (212 989 5566)
WEBSITE www.diacenter.org
OPEN Wednesday to Sunday, 12.00–18.00
SUBWAY 23rd Street C, E

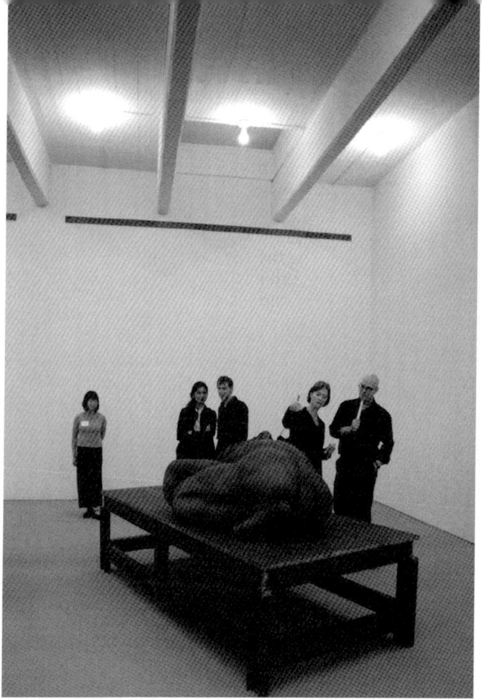

Feature Inc.

Say 'Feature' to anyone in New York's art world and a smile will automatically appear on their face as they fondly think of the gallery's dynamic founder, who goes by the sole name of Hudson. Like Madonna or Prince, this enigmatic character has a personality that precedes him. Hudson had worked in the non-profit sector for 12 years, but by the early 1980s became disgruntled with roster-oriented galleries. He himself used to create art, but ceased doing so in 1990.

The gallery was originally established in Chicago in 1984 and relocated to Broome Street in Manhattan in 1988. Its next stop was on Greene Street, before following the flock to Chelsea.

Hudson's approach to selecting artists is unconventional: he shows interesting work by artists who are not thoroughly established in the system. Moreover, he refuses to represent the artists that he works with, preferring to remain a stepping stone for young careers.

Instead of issuing the standard press release in conjunction with exhibitions, Hudson maintains his unorthodox approach to the art world by publishing a short interview with each artist. Conducting these interviews himself, the result is insightful without being judgemental. Rather like Feature Inc. itself.

ADDRESS 530 West 25th Street, New York, NY 10001 (212 675 7772)
OPEN Tuesday to Saturday, 11.00–18.00
SUBWAY 23rdStreet C, E

Feature Inc.

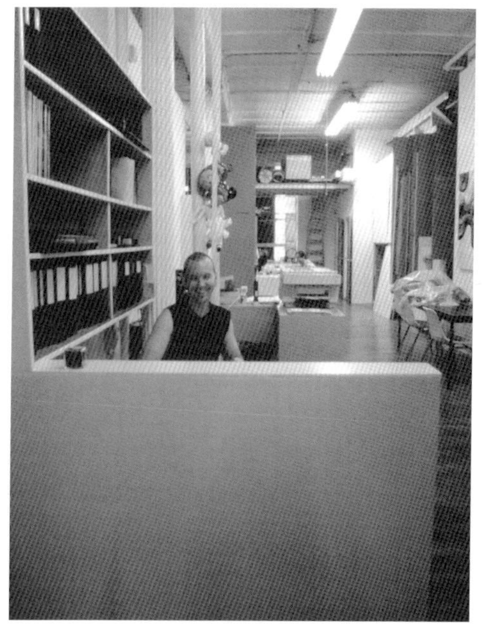

Feigen Contemporary

Feigen Contemporary has found its perfect home among the sleek and spacious new galleries that populate Chelsea. A spin off of Richard L Feigen & Co – an uptown gallery that exhibits masters from the fourteenth to the twentieth centuries – Feigen Contemporary is dedicated to presenting work by emerging, mid-career and well-established practising artists. Its eponymous founder began dealing in Chicago, and moved his enterprise to New York in 1963. Feigen was the first to show the work of Joseph Beuys in America.

The contemporary programme was initiated in 1989 by Lance Kinz, president and director of Feigen Contemporary. He was joined by Susan Reynolds as co-director in 1993. Both began operating the business from Chicago, then moved directly into Chelsea in 1997 after realising that more collectors pass through New York than detour north-west towards the Windy City. It also allowed them to run a more effective gallery from the epicentre of the international art market.

Many of the artists they represented in Chicago are still looked after in New York. In addition they present the work of Gregory Green, Chantal Joffe and James Rosenquist. Kinz and Reynolds have a good eye for emerging artists; Peter Garfield's photographs of model houses flying through the air and Jeremy Blake's morphing DVD projections were highlights of the 1999 programme.

ADDRESS 535 West 20th Street (212 929 0500)
OPEN Tuesday to Saturday, 11.00–18.00
SUBWAY 23rd Street C, E

Feigen Contemporary

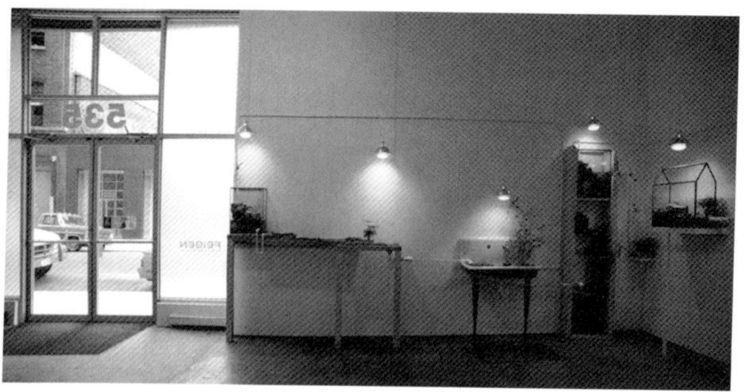

Jessica Fredericks Gallery

You could easily miss the nondescript façade of this basement gallery on 20th Street, set among the huge spaces for which Chelsea is notorious. But Jessica Fredericks is a virtual Aladdin's cave of burgeoning talent.

The space is run by husband-and-wife team Jessica Fredericks and Andrew Freiser. Andrew was an independent curator who organised shows at various places including Apex Art. Jessica came from a commercial background, doing time at Gagosian, Andre Emmerich, and Jose Frere. They represent a range of artists and frequently host group shows. *Pleasure Dome* in 1999 was a brilliant example, where Cathy de Monchaux's tiny sculpture of dancing frogs with erect penises was displayed alongside Richard Kern's pseudo-pornography and Marnie Weber's fairy-like collage of naked breasts collated from Japanese porn magazines.

Later-generation artists are also accommodated, such as John Wesley and the late Robert Overby. The latter was better known as a graphic designer who became a respected collector in LA. It was only after his death that his wife mounted a retrospective exhibition of the work he created in private and he was given the recognition he deserves; conceptually, the work is on a par with that of Richard Serra and Bruce Nauman.

Jessica Fredericks is also the home of rising star Michael Bevilacqua. A post-pop colourful melange of references, Bevilacqua's canvases mix references from high and low culture. From Matthew Barney to soap ads, there is nothing that Bevilacqua can't assimilate into his work. It seems as though there isn't anything that Jessica Fredericks can't successfully assimilate either.

ADDRESS 504 West 22nd Street, New York, NY 10011 (212 633 6555)
OPEN Tuesday to Saturday, 11.00–18.00
SUBWAY 23rd Street C, E

Jessica Fredericks Gallery

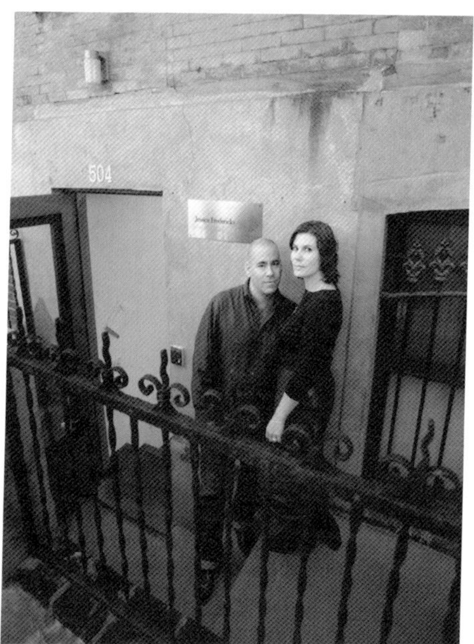

Barbara Gladstone Gallery

Stepping into Barbara Gladstone's super-chic gallery is like walking into a set for a film about the art world. Its dramatic space and immaculate white walls embody the ultimate cliché of the postmodern gallery.

Gladstone had to leave her previous space in Soho when the landlords made it impossible for her to renew the lease. More and more commercial ventures were moving into the area, and only corporations like The Gap, Pottery Barn and Victoria's Secret could afford the skyrocketing rents. Gladstone joined forces with Matthew Marks and Metro Pictures to buy the building on West 24th Street now colloquially known as MGM.

Gladstone represents some extremely interesting artists. Her selection spans generations and nationalities: she has a proficient eye for talent. Take, for example, the Iranian artist Shirin Neshat, whose photographs of women in traditional black headdress with Arabic writing superimposed on their skin hark back to the aggressiveness of the women's movementof the 1970s. A video by Neshat was a highlight of the 1999 Venice Biennale. German artist Rosemary Trockel also explores issues of gender relations in her work, which ranges from video to photography, painting and installation, and now commands top prices.

Los Angeles-based Lari Pittman's hallucinogenic paintings embrace pop culture, urbanism, gay life and the media. His work is perfect for Gladstone's space, which lends itself to large and colourful paintings. Matthew Barney, winner of the first Hugo Boss Prize, has had a meteoric rise to fame with Gladstone, who produces his films.

Barney's video series (called Cremaster after the muscles located in the male testicles) ranges in subject matter from spaced-out galactic cheerleaders prancing on a football field to a satyr who tap-dances at the bottom of the ocean. Each of the videos in the series employ psychedelic and hypnotic imagery so lush that watching them feels like being in a

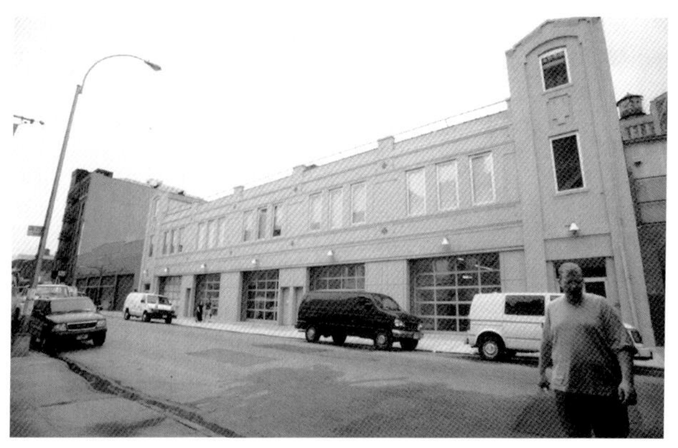

dream. His latest work, shot in grand locations (including the opera house) in Budapest, stars the aging but still exquisite Ursula Andress. Barney's talent for creating sumptuous imagery has lead to international acclaim.

More established artists represented by Gladstone include Vito Acconci, the legendary performance and video pioneer, and Richard Prince, whose joke paintings are the perfect anecdote to conceptual art.

ADDRESS 515 West 24th Street, New York, NY 10011 (212 206 9300)
OPEN Tuesday to Saturday, 10.00–18.00
SUBWAY 23rd Street C, E

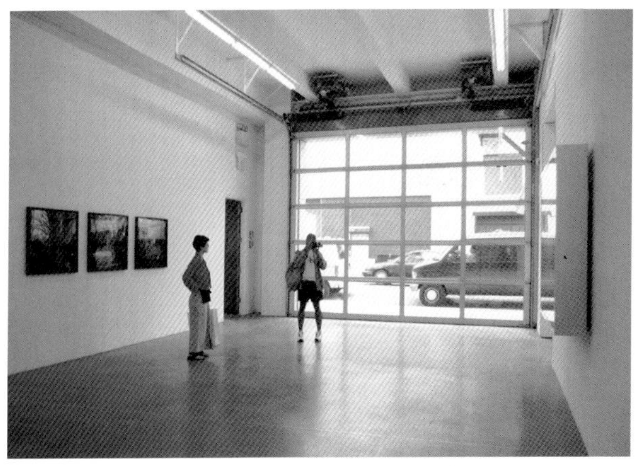

Klemens Gasser & Tanja Grunert, Inc.

Located on the same street as The Kitchen, Klemens Gasser & Tanja Grunert, Inc. takes one by surprise. No. 524 is not your average, glass-fronted, slick Chelsea space. First, there is no façade. A long concrete ramp built into the architecture of the building beckons visitors into the space. The loading ramp remains as evidence of the building's industrial history. Open to the elements, one marvels at the low security level of the gallery. The interior is similarly surprising. It has a slightly unfinished look, with wood beams that highlight the unique architectural features of the building.

Klemens Gasser and Tanja Grunert both came from Germany before setting up shop in New York. Grunert began with her own gallery in Stuttgart before relocating to Cologne. Gasser's story was similar, beginning with a gallery in Bozen, Italy, and finally ending up in Cologne. In autumn 1996 they joined forces to open a gallery in Cologne, then moved to the new space in New York in October 1998.

While it is a commercial space, the attitude of the gallery seems to belong more to an artist-run or publicly funded institution. They represent artists who appeal less to the media and more to the cognoscenti of the cutting-edge art world. These artists are international and span generations, ranging from feminist Austrian performance artist Valie Export to the Czech photographer Jitka Hanzlová. Günther Brus, Thomas Locher and Peter Zimmermann are also among those represented.

Gasser & Grunert have quietly achieved success with their selection of artists. Eija-Liisa Ahtila represented her native Finland in the 1999 Venice Biennale. One of the most exciting artists to come out of Scandinavia recently, her innovative video work was also shown in 1997's *Manifesta* in Luxembourg. Spanish-born Julio Rondo, who now lives in Germany, had a critically and commercially lauded show in spring 1999.

Klemens Gasser & Tanja Grunert, Inc.

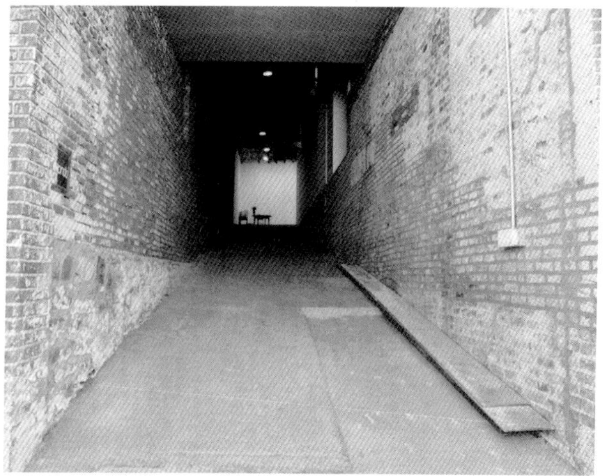

Klemens Gasser & Tanja Grunert, Inc.

4.30

Working within the tradition of painting, Rondo interpreted reality through a process of abstraction in two-piece geometric paintings. Despite their formal austerity, Rondo's work is based on still-lifes, portraits, landscapes and even political allegories.

ADDRESS 524 West 19th Street, New York, NY 10011 (212 807 9494)
OPEN Tuesday to Saturday, 10.00–18.00
SUBWAY West 18th Street 2, 9

Klemens Gasser & Tanja Grunert, Inc.

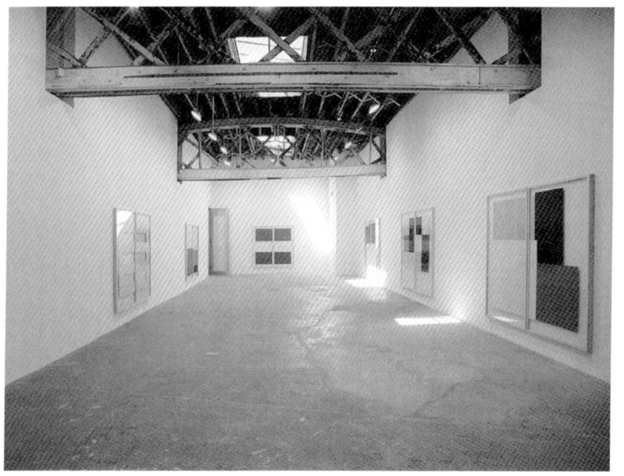

Greene Naftali

Greene Naftali represents the amalgamation of Carol Greene and Gloria Naftali. Five years old, it was the first gallery on this street and made Chelsea a neighbourhood of art spaces rather than just one strip on 22nd Street.

Carol Greene was formerly director of the now-defunct John Good Gallery in Soho, but Gloria Naftali does not have a history in the art world. She is owner of the massive building in which the gallery is located. The two met when Carol Greene was frantically looking at venues for a gallery. Naftali was particularly taken by Greene's choice of artists and offered her a partnership in exchange for use of the best space in the building.

Taking the elevator to the eighth floor, visitors wind their way through a bleak maze of corridors to arrive in a beautiful space with an impressive view through the north wall, almost completely covered by windows which allow plenty of natural light into the space. A huge iron sliding door – a unique architectural element – hides Naftali's office.

The gallery represents international artists including Alex Katz, Lucy Gunning, Jacqueline Humphries, and Daniel Pflumm. Greene and Naftali also host live performance and musical events at the gallery.

ADDRESS 8th floor, 526 West 26th Street, New York, NY 10001
(212 463 7770)
OPEN Tuesday to Saturday, 10.00–18.00
SUBWAY 23rd Street C, E

Greene Naftali

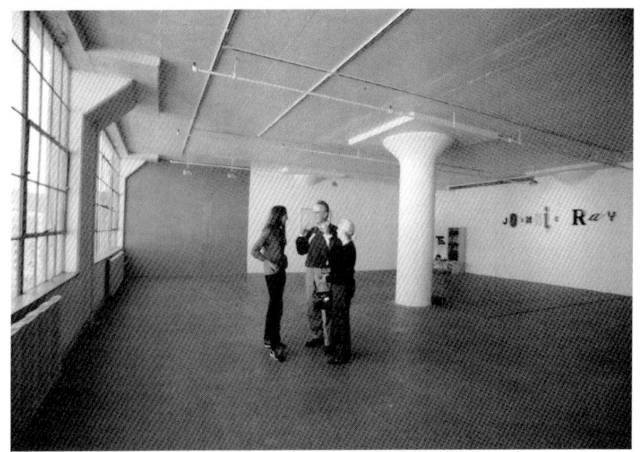

Pat Hearn

A fixture of the New York art world, Pat Hearn has weathered many storms during her career. Rhode Island born and bred, at the age of 30 the classy Hearn owned the hippest young gallery in Manhattan, located in Alphabet City within the East Village. In the mid 1980s this was not the trendy boutique district it is today – Alphabet City was known for drugs and crime, and Hearn's decision to settle there required some courage. But Hearn has always taken risks.

Hearn moved to New York in 1981, and sang in the jazz band Wild and Wonderful while hoping to establish herself as an artist and a dealer. She opened a gallery in 1983 but soon realised that she could not straddle the domains of both art production and dealing, and so ceased creating her own work. It was during this period that she met Colin Deland, founder of American Fine Arts, who became her husband in 1999.

Hearn relocated to Chelsea in 1994, during the period in which her mates Paul Morris and Matthew Marks also arrived here. The new space embodies the more grown-up taste of Hearn. A façade featuring opague windows catches the attention of passers-by. Just what is inside this mysterious space, where neighbours such as the Comme des Garçons shop and the Dia Center for the Arts attract hundreds? Inside Hearn's gallery one will find a polished space that shows some of the best of contemporary art. The paintings of Mary Heilmann, Jutta Koether and Monique Prieto are sold here. She also shows prominent video artists Renee Green and Joan Jonas.

Hearn's is a success story, but she has not always been blessed with good fortune. When diagnosed with liver cancer in 1997, Hearn had complications with her health insurer, who would not pay for the treatment. Her friends in the art world rallied in support. Paul Morris organised a benefit auction to raise money for treatment of her illness.

Pat Hearn

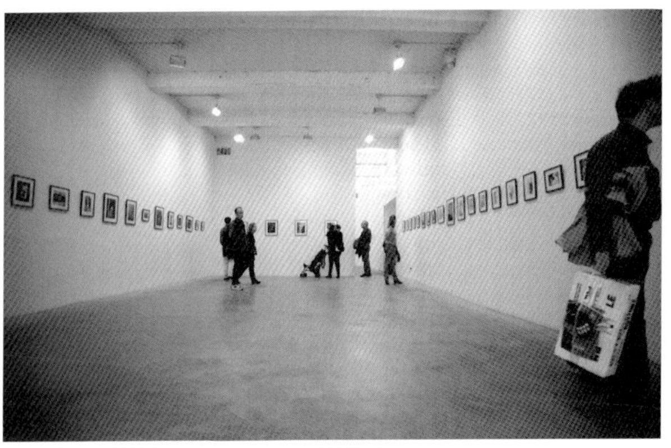

Pat Hearn

Returning with a renewed vigour, Hearn became one of the founders of The Armory Fair (see page 5.2). In fact it was her idea to stage the Gramercy Art Fair after she had been invited to similar events in Europe, but couldn't afford to travel to them. Perhaps not surprisingly, her fair is fast becoming one of the most important events on the contemporary art-world's calendar.

ADDRESS 530 West 22nd Street, New York, NY 10011 (212 727 7366)
OPEN Tuesday to Saturday, 11.00–18.00
SUBWAY 23rd Street C, E

Pat Hearn

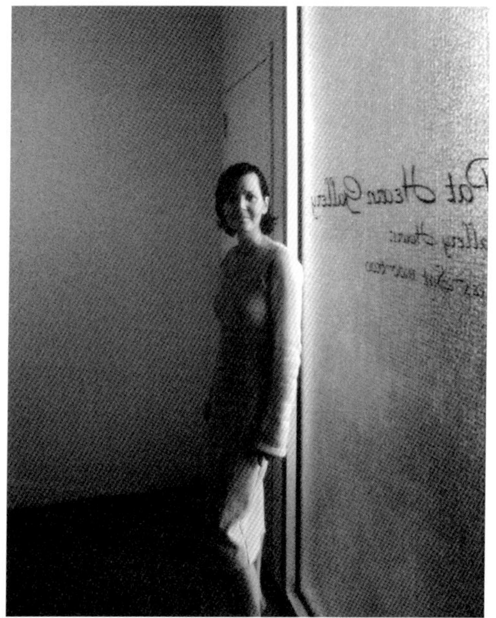

Paul Kasmin

Like Sean Kelly, David McKee and Gavin Brown, Paul Kasmin is an example of a Brit-done-well in the American art world. For those familiar with London's art scene, the name Kasmin alone should give a clue to Paul's *haute*-bohemian heritage. His father was John Kasmin, the first dealer to show David Hockney in London.

Paul Kasmin's introduction at an early age to the elite of 1960s swinging London instilled in him confidence in his own taste and vision. This is reflected in the artists he represents. He took chances with painters Elliot Puckette, Santi Moix and Walton Ford. Yet these turned up trumps for Kasmin as they, alongside Aaron Rose, James Nares and Nancy Rubins, are all rising art stars. Kasmin has proved his dedication to his artists by placing their work in important private and public collections.

Kasmin came to America because of a love of photography that was not matched commercially back in Britain. His first gallery opened in the early 1980s on Lower Broadway with a well-received show of Brancusi photographs. The intimacy of that space and Kasmin's personable personality was what led some of the artists whom he still represents to join him – Donald Baechler was one of these. But a need for more space brought him to Grand Street in 1989. Ten years later came the inevitable relocation to Chelsea.

ADDRESS 293 Tenth Avenue, New York, NY 10001 (212 563 4474)
OPEN Tuesday to Saturday, 10.00–18.00
SUBWAY 25th Street C, E

Paul Kasmin

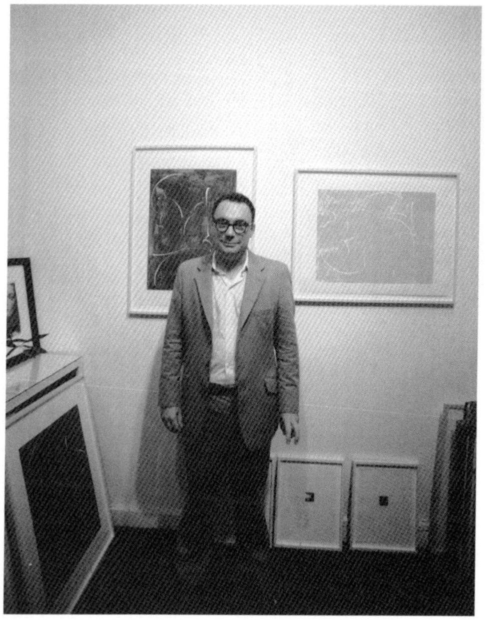

The Kitchen

The Kitchen is an interdisciplinary centre for emerging and established artists. It has existed in its space on 19th Street since the 1970s, long before the Soho galleries made a mass exodus to Chelsea.

With two theatres, an art gallery and mini-canteen, The Kitchen offers a variety of entertainment at any one time. One can see a dance or theatre performance, and combine this with a visit to the gallery, which is essentially a small foyer adjacent to a black-box theatre.

Established in 1971, The Kitchen has always showcased cutting-edge technology. Hip to the latest DJs, performance art and interactive discussion, The Kitchen has been known to collaborate with other publicly funded institutions. A few years ago they joined forces with The Institute of Contemporary Arts in London, digitally linking up and hosting a live concert with musicians on both continents jamming simultaneously and broadcasting over the net.

The Kitchen hosts an annual Summer Institute, with workshops on disciplines ranging from scriptwriting to yoga, voice and dance. In 1999 a complementary series of public talks featured such eminent figures as Laurie Anderson, Philip Glass and Meredith Monk.

ADDRESS 512 West 19th Street, New York, NY 10011 (212 255 5793)
WEBSITE www.thekitchen.org
OPEN gallery open one hour before performances, and every Saturday, 12.00–18.00
SUBWAY 18th Street 1, 9

The Kitchen

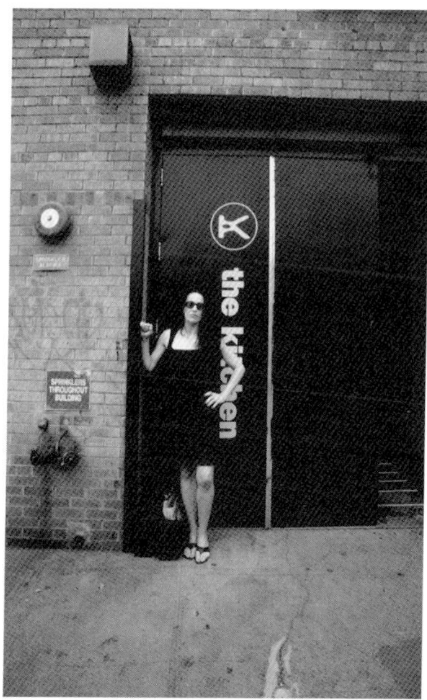

Matthew Marks

It is only a matter of time before the name Matthew Marks will be on a par with the Gagosians and Boones of the international art world. The rise of this 38-year-old New Yorker, who had collected a thousand prints by nineteenth- and twentieth-century American artists by the time he was 18, has already been meteoric. It was his eye for that at-the-time not so lucrative market for prints that allowed Marks to make his mark as a mainstream dealer. During a year off from college spent at Pace Wildenstein he curated a print show that quickly established his reputation.

A brief interlude at Anthony D'Offay Gallery in London helped him to forge relationships with many important collectors and artists, including Lucien Freud, whose print work Marks is solely responsible for. This backdoor tactic – acquiring artists by first representing their print work – later helped Marks lure Brice Marden away from Mary Boone.

By the time he returned to New York Marks was ready to open his own gallery, which he did salon-style in his uptown apartment on Madison Avenue. (Marks was no stranger to the Upper East Side as his father was CEO and president of Memorial Sloan Kettering Hospital.) After seven years Marks was in need of a more versatile space; the townhouse could not accommodate large works. It was Marks' admiration for the Dia Centre (see page 4.10), that led him to Chelsea.

Marks fell in love with a space originally used as an ambulance garage. The landlords could not understand what Marks wanted with such a building, but after a year of negotiation and renovation Matthew Marks Gallery opened its doors in October 1994 as the first commercial gallery in Chelsea. The inaugural show was Ellsworth Kelly. Marks' opening-night fear that nobody would attend was soon shifted to the safety of the art on the walls as more than a thousand people crammed into the gallery.

When Marks opened his space he wrote to all of his favorite artists

Matthew Marks

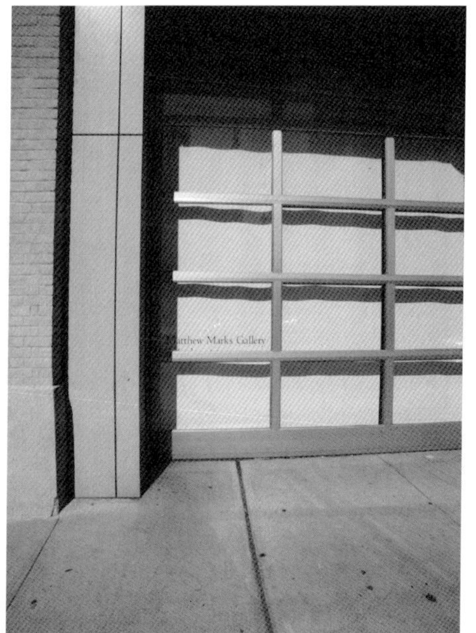

asking them to consider showing their work. Gary Hume, Terry Winters, Louise Bourgeious, and Nan Goldin were among the recipients of these letters. It was only a year later that Nan Goldin joined him. Marks has a knack for courting artists. He introduced Goldin to her long-time hero Marden and escorted her on trips to Venice and Vienna. Gary Hume has since joined his roster, alongside internationally recognised names such as Peter Fischli/David Weiss, Andreas Gursky, Roni Horn and Sam Taylor-Wood.

Between 1995 and 1997 a new gallery moved into Chelsea almost every week. Marks found he needed even more space, and became the first to have two galleries in Chelsea. He joined forces with Barbara Gladstone, who was literally on the street because her Soho landlords would not renew her lease (see page 4.24). Together they found a suitable building on 24th Street, which they also share with Metro Pictures. This disused knife factory is now one of the most important locations for contemporary art in New York. With Luhring Augustine and Andrea Rosen recently arrived as neighbours, this block has become the focus of powerhouse dealing in Chelsea.

ADDRESS 522 West 22nd Street; 523 West 24th Street, New York, NY 10011 (212 243 0200)
OPEN Tuesday to Saturday, 10.00–18.00
SUBWAY 23rd Street C, E

Matthew Marks

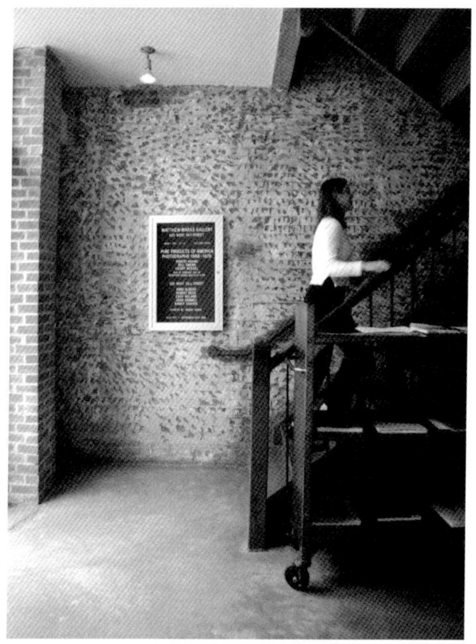

Metro Pictures

The merger of the ideas, experience, personalities and passions of Helene Winer and Jannelle Reiring is what makes Metro Pictures. Winer and Reiring, the founding directors who opened the gallery in Soho in 1980, have since been joined by Tom Heman. Winer had been director of Artists' Space and Reiring learned the business by working for Leo Castelli. Winer's experience in working with emerging artists proved absolutely essential for the first few years of Metro Pictures. They have now filled the shoes of their former employers and many young dealers have done time at Metro Pictures before opening their own galleries.

Metro Pictures is one of three galleries for contemporary art that share a transformed two-storey warehouse in Chelsea. Although they had not originally planned to move from their Greene Street space, Winer and Reiring jumped at the opportunity that was presented to them. Joining forces with Barbara Gladstone, who needed to move from the hyper-inflated rents of Soho, and Matthew Marks, the young dealer who was looking to expand his space, the team purchased a building on 24th Street in a mutually beneficial arrangement: Metro Pictures and Barbara Gladstone share the street level while Marks enjoys a vast space upstairs.

The conversion was designed by Michael Kostow of Kapell and Kostow Architects. His brief was to allow more flexibility in the gallery space, and to lower the floor, which had been elevated several feet for its use as a loading dock. Kostow's solution included converting the garage-type doors into large windows that could be rolled up and down. This allowed natural light to enter the gallery space, and provided the advantage of easy access for installation. Now trucks with loads of heavy and unwieldy art can drive straight into the gallery space. (These doors were first conceived for Matthew Marks' original gallery on 22nd Street.)

The 30,000-square-foot building is occupied primarily by Gladstone

Metro Pictures

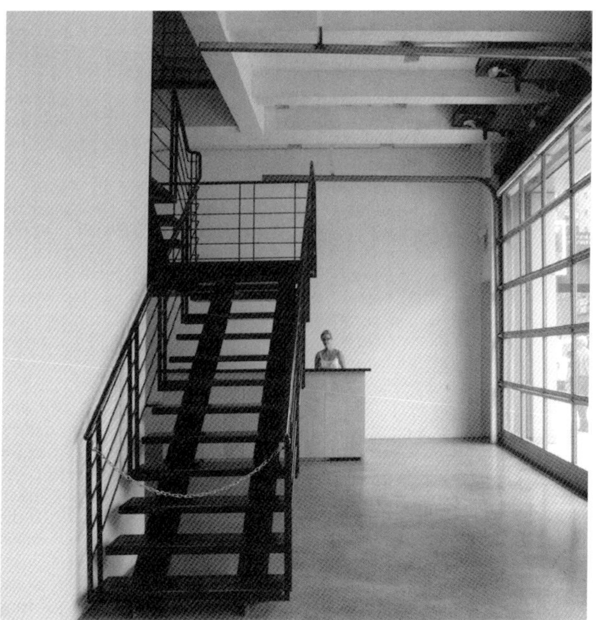

and Metro Pictures. Winer and Reiring's galleries are set back from the street. The first thing a visitor encounters when walking through the door is an expansive reception space with a large stairwell. The galleries, sheltered from passers-by, show work by some of the most established artists in the contemporary international market. Cindy Sherman, whose obsession with depicting herself in various guises has made her an artworld household name, is part of the Metro lineup. Tony Oursler, an artist who cleverly incorporates video and sound into sculpture, has joined the ranks. Fred Wilson, deeply interested in the things that people collect, is another artist represented. Add to this Ronald Jones, Robert Longo and Laurie Simmons and you have an extremely impressive lineup.

Winer and Reiring opened the gallery based entirely on the strength of a group of young artists who at the time had little exposure and were in need of representation. They have always maintained that their job as dealers is to exploit and enlarge existing interest in artists, rather than to create interest in the first place. Ironically, they are now in a position to create instant interest in whomsoever they deem worthy.

ADDRESS 519 West 24th Street, New York, NY 10011 (212 206 7100)
OPEN Tuesday to Saturday, 10.00–18.00
SUBWAY 23rd Street C, E

Metro Pictures

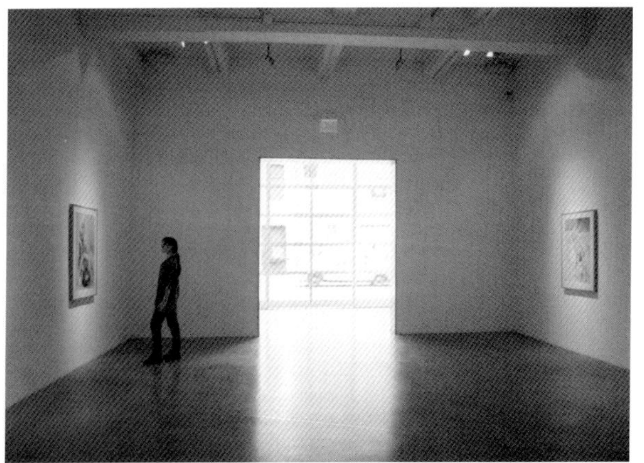

Paul Morris Gallery

Paul Morris Gallery is dwarfed by many of the monumental and ostentatious spaces in newly sophisticated Chelsea. However, this understated and classy gallery holds its own against its larger rivals, combining an unintimidating atmosphere with a line-up of international artists.

The gallery specialises in photography and drawing, with most of the work shown being flat and kept in files. Artists represented include Australian Tracey Moffatt, American Mary Beyt, and German photographer Oliver Boberg. Morris also deals in the secondary market, with works that include drawings by Willem de Kooning.

Morris has worked as far afield as Anthony D'Offay Gallery in London, and has been involved in a number of successful commercial ventures in Manhattan. He was co-owner, with Pat Hearn and Thomas Healy, of a gallery on West 22nd Street. He and Healy then ran the Morris Healy Gallery. The current location, on the ground floor of the landmark building The London Terrace must be an asset when it comes to attracting the appropriate clientele.

Morris is also well known for his role in several key alternative art fairs in Manhattan. During the lean years of the post-crash art market, Morris and friends organised The Gramercy Show, an art fair held in a hotel (see page 5.2). Once the market picked up again, Morris, Pat Hearn, Matthew Marks and Colin Deland organised the Armory Show, an art fair held in the famous building on Park Avenue. Morris and his colleagues played a major part in reviving the waning New York art market.

ADDRESS 465 West 23rd Street, New York, NY 10011 (212 727 2752/ pmgallery@mindspring.com)
OPEN Tuesday to Saturday, 11.00–18.00
SUBWAY 23rd Street C, E

Paul Morris Gallery

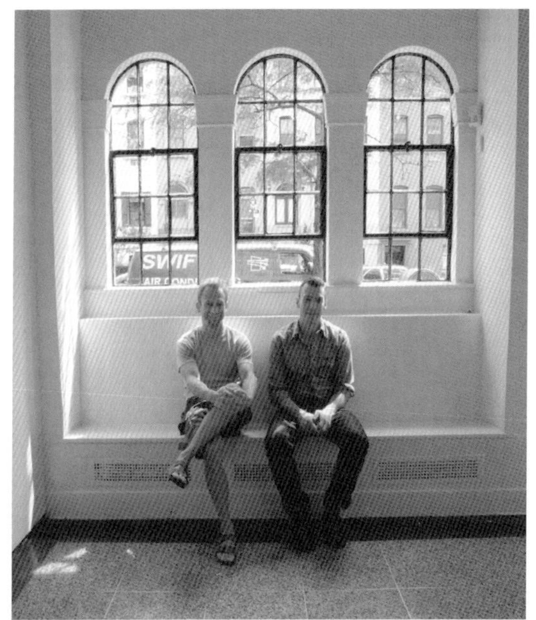

Postmasters Gallery

Postmasters Gallery was founded by Magdalena Sawon and Tamas Banovich in 1984. It has arrived at its current location after five years in the East Village and another nine on Greene Street in Soho. Unlike some of the neighbouring spaces in the newly 'discovered' area of Chelsea, Postmasters has an unassuming and uncorporate quality. Sawon and Banovich fully intend this as they are adamant that the space take its character from the art rather than the other way around.

Postmasters has gained a reputation for showing solid rather than of-the-moment work, although much of it is conceptual. Conceptual feminist pioneer Mary Kelly is one of their veteran artists. Sylvia Kolbowski, Janine Antoni and Paul Ramirez Jonas are also on the roster. They are complemented by a group of impressive emerging names such as Swiss artist Sylvie Fleury and ex-fashion model turned artist Mariko Mori from Japan.

459 West 19th Street was formerly a garage. Its façade remains as evidence of its banal history. However, the 15-foot ceilings and skylights give it a distinctly sophisticated appearance that enhances the directors' commitment to showing art concerned with new technologies. The absence of a visible reception desk is a welcome relief for visitors who normally feel scrutinised by the over-eager eyes of gallery staff.

ADDRESS 459 West 19 Street, New York, NY 10011 (212 727 3323)
OPEN Tuesday to Saturday, 11.00–18.00
SUBWAY 23rd Street N, R

Postmasters Gallery

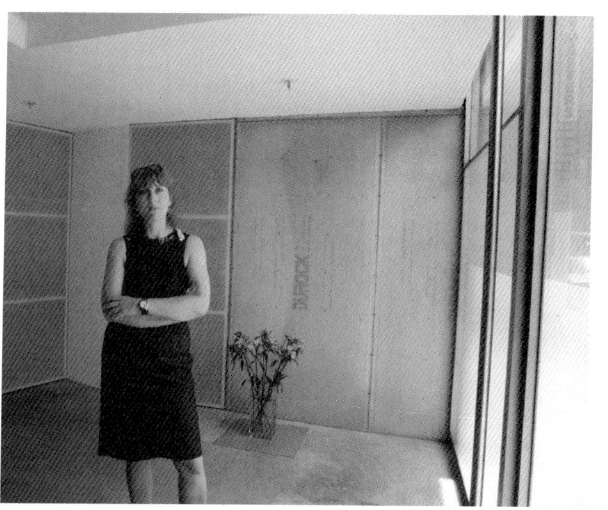

Max Protetch

Max Protetch is always doing the right thing at the right time. Since he opened his first gallery at the tender age of 23 in 1969, Protetch has consistently shown a high standard of work from disciplines within the fine arts and architecture. He opened the first gallery in Washington while pursuing a graduate degree at Georgetown University. Here Protetch represented Andy Warhol and other pop artists as well as the conceptual artists Sol LeWitt, Joseph Kosuth and On Kawara. Donald Judd, Dan Flavin, Lawrence Weiner and Carl Andre also exhibited during the 1970s and Protetch gave Vito Acconci his first one-man show. *Political Art* was a particularly memorable – and timely – show that dealt with the Marxist and political/economic involvements of minimal and conceptual art and included work by Daniel Buren, Dorothea Rockburne and Robert Morris. The subject came naturally to the dealer who was studying political science and economics.

His move to New York came in 1978. Protetch began to show architectural drawings, a genre that would become increasingly important to his gallery. Over the years he has shown work by many of the most applauded architects including Robert Venturi, Michael Graves, Peter Eisenmann, Zaha Hadid, Frank Gehry and Tadao Ando. Protech also represents the estates of Frank Lloyd Wright, Buckminster Fuller and the untimely departed Aldo Rossi. Last year Protetch commemorated the Italian maestro with an exhibition of drawings spanning his brief but influential career.

In the same vein Protetch supports artists who create works that fall outside the traditional media associated with fine art. Functional sculpture by Siah Armajani and Scott Burton is shown by Protetch. Likewise he has taken on ceramicists Betty Woodman and Richard DeVore, whose work comes out of the history of the vessel and shares many of the

Max Protetch

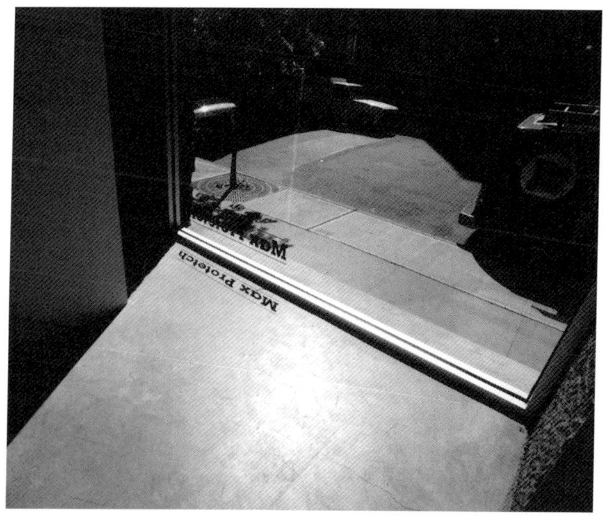

concerns of painting and sculpture. Oliver Herring, a young sculptor who knits out of sticky tape and other mundane materials, has found success at the gallery.

Proof of Max Protetch's ability to evolve over time is his recent commitment to Asian art. A new generation of Chinese artists was presented in two group shows in 1997/98. In 1999 artist Zhang Huan presented *Raising an Anonymous Mountain by One Metre*, which included ten nude people piled on top of one another. This piece, which is documented in video and photographic form, as also shown at the 1999 Venice Biennale.

Obviously, Protetch's net is cast wide. His interests are varied, but the work shown is always top quality. Protetch has a knack for going beyond commercial ventures and seeing the work for what it can be: a catalyst for discussion and discourse on contemporary culture.

ADDRESS 511 West 22nd Street, New York, NY 10011 (212 633 6999)
OPEN Tuesday to Saturday, 10.00–18.00
SUBWAY 23rd Street C, E

Andrea Rosen

What do Rita Ackermann, John Coplans, Sean Landers and Ken Lum all have in common? Besides being represented by Andrea Rosen, the factor that bonds them is their work which, although visually seductive, is preoccupied with the conceptual. Take, for example, John Currin, another member of Rosen's flock. His paintings have been widely celebrated and have even appeared on a Pulp album cover. His work has been described as a cross between Lucas Cranach and a Vargas pin-up. Although firmly placed in the contemporary, Currin's work embraces old-master techniques. His treatment of flesh (oozing from tight bodices) and hair blowing in an unseen breeze is reminiscent of Botticelli and Ingres.

Rosen is also responsible for the body of work that was left after the tragic and untimely death of Felix Gonzalez-Torres. Growing out of an interest in social activism, particularly the subjects of homosexuality and AIDS, Gonzalez-Torres's work managed to avoid an overtly political feel. With work such as *Untitled (USA Today)* (1990) the artist encouraged visitors to take a bonbon home with them from the pile that made up the installation. This represented more than just giving away candy. For Torres, it symbolised endless generosity and the hope of endless renewal and divine grace. This kind of work contrasted with the gay art of the previous decade, where homo-erotic imagery was the dominant aesthetic for Johns, Rauschenburg and Warhol.

Rosen's arists have been included in a number of prestigious exhibitions. Andrea Zittel, a young American artist whose work examines living spaces and ideal environments, participated in international exhibitions including a solo show at Sadie Coles in London and the 1997 Munster Sculpture Project. Here she showed 'Escape Vehicles', mini-caravans decorated by invited guests, including Miuccia Prada, who designed their ideal escape environment.

Andrea Rosen

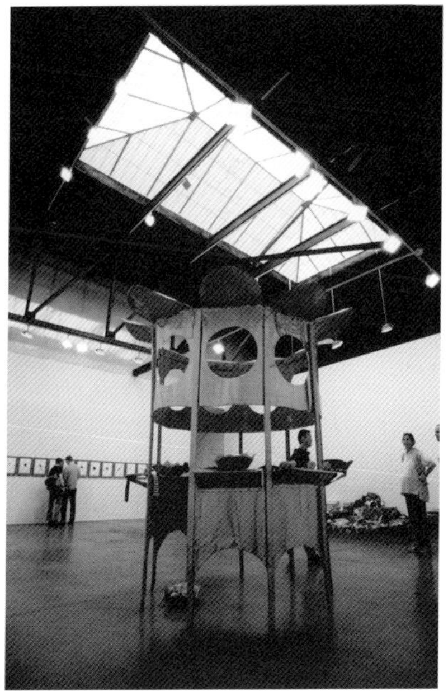

Andrea Rosen

Wolfgang Tillmans is also in Andrea Rosen's line-up. The young German photographer has received widespread acclaim for his work, which crosses the boundaries of commercial photography and fine art and who rose to prominence through the pages of London style magazines such as *The Face* and *i-D*.

Rosen's impressive choice of artists enables the gallery to lure an average of 2000 visitors a week. Initially reluctant, Rosen does not regret her move to Chelsea in 1998. Sharing the same building as Luhring Augustine, Rosen's space has the versatility of high ceilings and an expansive space. Her first gallery, opened in 1990 when Soho was still the epicentre of the art world, was located at 130 Prince Street. Rosen plans to extend her space and programme in 2000, moves which reflect her rapid ascent through the ranks of the New York art world.

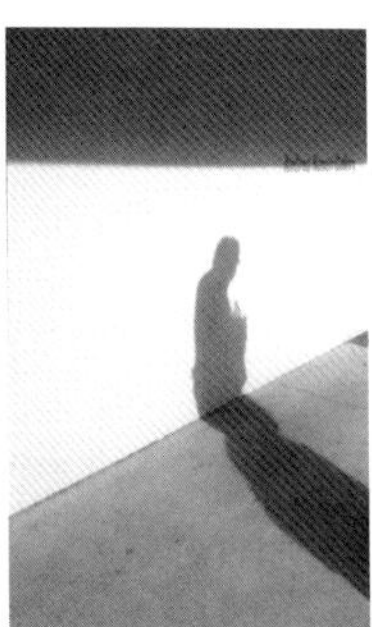

ADDRESS 525 West 24th Street, New York, NY 10011 (212 627 6000)
OPEN Tuesday to Saturday, 10.00–18.00
SUBWAY 23rd Street C, E

Andrea Rosen

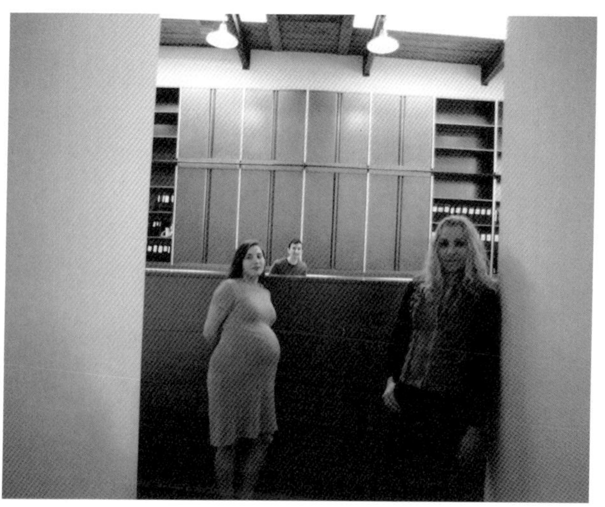

Jack Shainman

Shainman had more than his fair share of hiccups whilst establishing himself in this distinctively large (9000-square-foot), Chelsea site. Objections from homeless tramps, who had resided in the disused building for years, came after month-long negotiations with a landlord who simply could not understand why tenants, who were used to the amenities of Soho, would want an empty, cold shell without running water isolated in the desolate territory north of the Meat Packing District.

But you can't put a good man down. And Jack Shainman is certainly a good man. He made friends with the tramps and made use of the amenities down the street at No. 529. But that was all more than two years ago and once-derelict Chelsea is now virtually gentrified; the tramps have moved on, Shainman has installed a bathroom – and a beautiful bathroom it is too.

Artists that feature on his roster include Shimon Attie (who was responsible for the brilliantly conceived project with Creative Time; see page 8.2), Micah Lexier, whose sculptures are executed in one minute, and the rising art-world star Kerry James Marshall.

'I look for original artists who manage to balance the aesthetic with the conceptual', Shainman explains, 'but I choose from my heart as well as my mind.' The love of his brood is just about all they have in common with one another. Male, female, young and old (Betty Goodwin is already over 70), black and white, Americans and Europeans make his list read like a tribute to diversity.

ADDRESS 513 West 20th Street, New York, NY 10011 (212 645 1701)
OPEN Tuesday to Saturday, 11.00–18.00
SUBWAY 23rd Street C, E

Jack Shainman

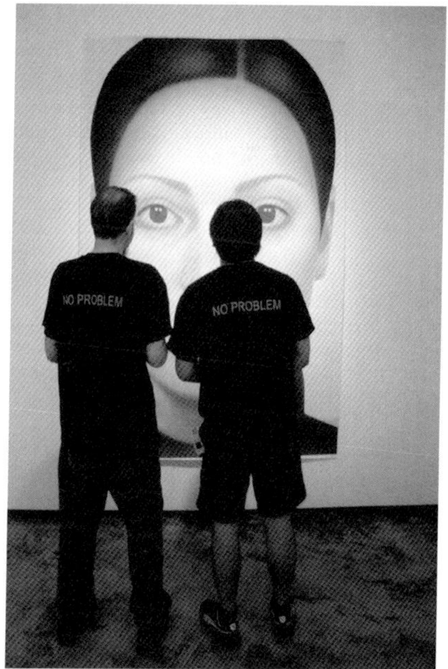

Sonnabend

Ileana Sonnabend is a remarkable woman. With almost six decades of dealing art under her belt, she is still always on the look-out for new young talent. Born in Romania, Ileana Sonnabend (*née* Schapira) met legendary art dealer Leo Castelli when she was only 17. Married one year later, they were eventually forced to flee Europe because of the Nazi occupation. With the relationship already disintegrating, Castelli served in Europe with the US Army. After an amicable split from Castelli, Ileana met Michael Sonnabend while studying psychology at Columbia University. In 1959 she married Michael only to move back to Europe in order to escape the New York art-world gossip.

Finally settling in Paris, the Sonnabends began acting as agents there for Robert Rauschenberg, who had previously had a notorious battle with Ileana's ex-husband. Sonnabend became famous for showing pop art, which brought them so much profit that they were able to open galleries in Geneva, Switzerland and New York where Sonnabend was bold enough to secure the space directly above her ex-husband's gallery at 420 West Broadway.

Within the walls of her New York space, artists were given free reign to do as they pleased. And they did. For example, in 'Seedbed', Vito Acconci hid under the floorboards and masturbated continually. In the 1980s Jeff Koons showed paintings and sculptures of himself and his new bride, Italian porn-queen-cum-politician Cicciolina, in pornographic poses. Artists were drawn to work with Ileana because of this excessively liberal attitude.

In the new millennium Sonnabend launched a new headquarters in New York. Joining the rest of their colleagues, Sonnabend has relocated to a ground-floor space in Chelsea. Keeping with the ideology that helped establish her gallery, Ileana represents a mixed bag of artists. From the

Sonnabend

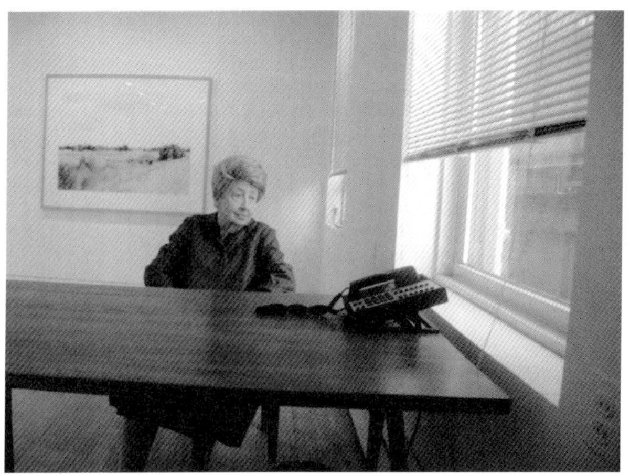

original artists represented, such as Robert Rauschenberg and Gilbert & George to conceptual great John Baldessari and minimalist Robert Morris, to newer acquisitions such as Peter Halley, Sonnabend has kept her commitment to go fearlessly where no other dealer has gone before. Ileana Sonnabend is without doubt one of the most powerful art dealers in the world today.

ADDRESS The Eagle Building, 536 West 22nd Street, New York, NY 10011 (212 966 6160)
OPEN see *Gallery Guide*
TRANSPORT 23rd Street C, E

Sonnabend

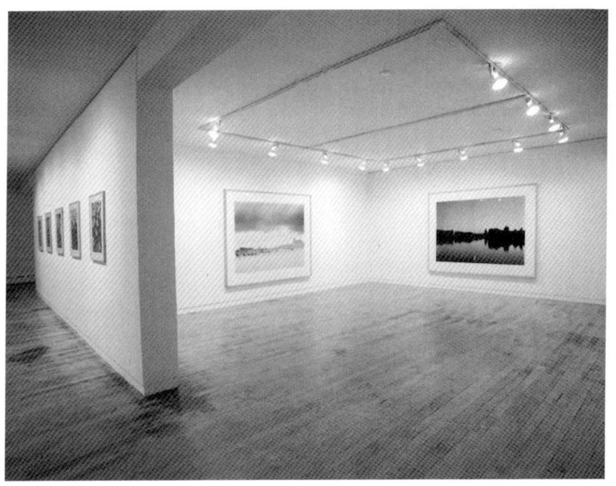

White Columns

White Columns is New York's oldest alternative space. And if this isn't reason enough to make it worth visiting, the fact that it was founded by Gordon Matta-Clark and Jeffrey Lew should give it further pulling power.

They started the gallery as an experimental exhibition space in 1969 at 112 Greene Street in Soho and named it 112 Workshop. It was only when the organisation moved to Spring Street a decade later that it became known, as it is today, as White Columns. A further move in 1991 took them to Christopher Street in the West Village and then in 1998 they finally put down roots at the current space on the borders of the Village and the Meat Packing District where they are attracting more than 1200 visitors a month.

Matta-Clark and Lew set up the gallery as a not-for-profit space that would provide a platform for the best work being done by emerging and under-supported artists. This mandate still stands today and has launched the career of many of America's most prominent artists. Obviously Gordon Matta-Clark comes high on this list, as does William Wegman, Alice Aycock and more recently Lorna Simpson, Andres Serrano, Cady Noland, Sean Landers and John Currin.

The quality of the artists showing had an instant impact on the reputation of White Columns. As they grew in prestige, so more and more young artists approached the gallery for help and advice. Unlike many other galleries, White Columns accepts and reviews slide submissions all season and makes studio visits with hundreds of artists all year. This gargantuan task is overseen by executive director Paul Ha who also found time in the last two years to curate *In My Room* (where artists such as Alyson Levy and Suzanne Wright created fantasy worlds in which they could operate), and *Journey* (a group exhibition of young artists performing feats of endurance).

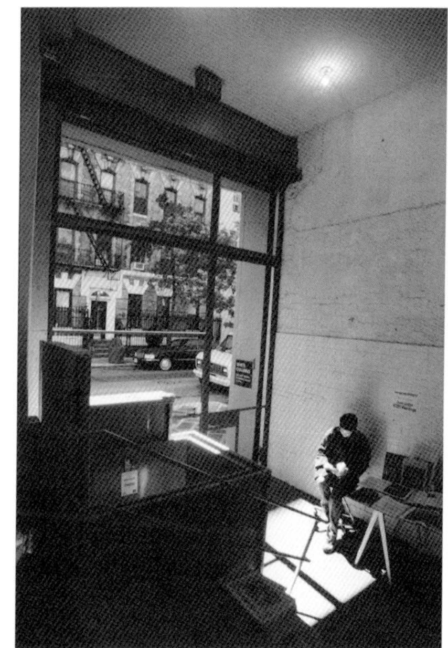

White Columns

Part of Ha's job is to personally meet and advise more than 800 artists each year. Artists who have already submitted work to the Slide File may be given an opportunity to exhibit in New York. Through this unparalleled programme White Columns shows the work of approximately 200 artists every year and meets with many more. The Slide File includes work by more than 2000 artists and is frequently used by curators, writers and dealers looking for new art.

Running alongside this is the exhibition programme. It is made up of main gallery shows, which include thematic group shows and commissioned installations, and the White Room Program, which is a series of introductory solo shows by emerging artists who have no gallery representation in New York.

White Columns has built an unmatched reputation for integrity and provided a much-needed starting point for young artists. It was the first of its kind and continues to be at the forefront of launching young talent.

ADDRESS 320 West 13th Street, New York, NY 10014 (212 924 4212)
WEBSITE www.whitecolumns.org
OPEN Wednesday to Sunday, 12.00–18.00
SUBWAY 14th Street A, C, E, L

White Columns

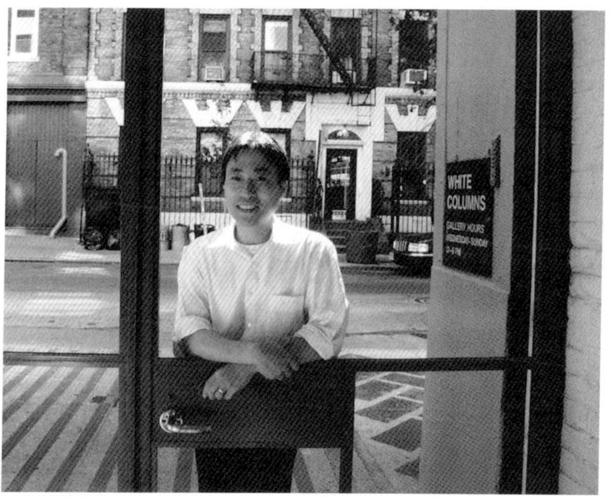

hell's kitchen

The Armory Show (The International Fair of New Art) 5.2

The Armory Show (The International Fair of New Art)

More than 70 of the world's top art dealers descended on New York in February 1999 to show their wares to all who wandered through the grand entrance of the 69th Regiment Armory.

This event was born out of necessity after five years of leaning paintings on walls, hanging photos from shower curtains and fear of what was under the bed at the Gramercy Park Hotel. The hotel had been the location of the Gramercy International Contemporary Art Fair since 1994 when Pat Hearn, Matthew Marks, Paul Morris and Colin De Land had grouped together to form an art fair for New York, based on a hotel fair that Hearn had heard about in Amsterdam. The market was ripe for it; the recession had pushed prices down and young dealers representing young artists could not afford the prices of the Art Dealers Association of America's (ADAA) blue-chip show (around $20,000 per stall), held uptown at the 7th Regiment Armory on Park Avenue. But the cheap room hire finally became more hindrance than help. The small rooms could not house the work nor hold the droves of people that passed through them as the Gramercy Art Fair became the most popular of (and the model for) all hotel fairs across the United States.

Moving to the 69th Regiment Armory made more than sense. This venue had the added kudos of being the location of one of America's most controversial art fairs way back in 1913. Officially titled *The International Exhibition of Modern Art* but better known simply as 'The Armory Show', it was the single most important art exhibition ever held in the USA, significant both for its size – it included about 1300 pieces of art – and because its message dramatically changed the course of American art. Organised and financed by artists, many of the pieces were included to educate an American audience about modern European painters. Goya,

The Armory Show (The International Fair of New Art)

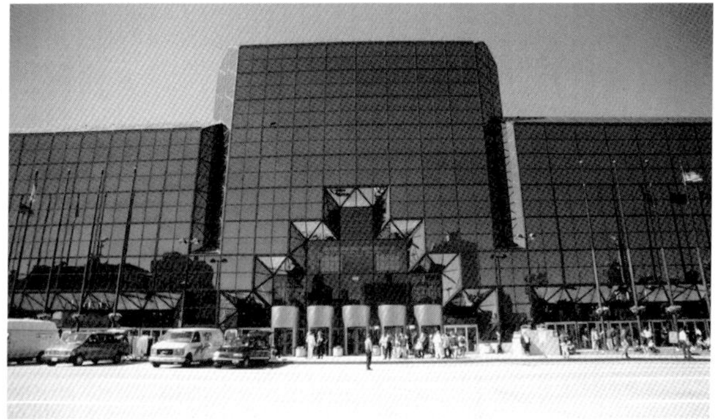

The Armory Show (The International Fair of New Art)

Delacroix, Degas, Manet, Monet, Van Gogh, Picasso and Gaugin were all shown for the first time in the USA. But it was Marcel Duchamp's 'Nude Descending a Staircase', characterised as 'an explosion in a shingle factory', that caused a stir.

The 1999 show finally put the downtown dealers on a par with their uptown brethren. They cunningly decided to hold their show on the same weekend as the ADAA held theirs, knowing that the blue-chip collectors would not miss an opportunity to make one stop downtown and see what was on offer. The weekend was opened with an evening preview benefit for the Dia Center for the Arts. Dealers came from as far afield as London (White Cube and Interim Art), Amsterdam (Torch), Germany (Jablonka, Neu), Austria, Belgium, Japan, Los Angeles and Chicago.

Success meant that the 69th Regiment Armory simply couldn't contain all the galleries which wanted space for 2000. So the four founding dealers and the show's director, Tom Delavan, moved the first show of the new millennium to the New North Pavilion at the Javits Convention Center.

Now an annual event, the Amory Show is unpredictable, exciting and immense fun. Whether you are there to buy, art-world star-spot (former gallery owner John McEnroe has been seen doing the rounds with David Zwirner), or simply be inspired by new art you will not be disappointed, as year by year this show emerges as America's most important for both emerging artists and dealers.

ADDRESS New North Pavilion, Jacob Javits Convention Center, 11th and 12th Avenues between 34th and 39th Streets, New York (212 777 3338/ armoryshow@hotmail.com)
OPEN held annually in February; check listing magazines for hours
SUBWAY 34th Street A, C, E

The Armory Show (The International Fair of New Art)

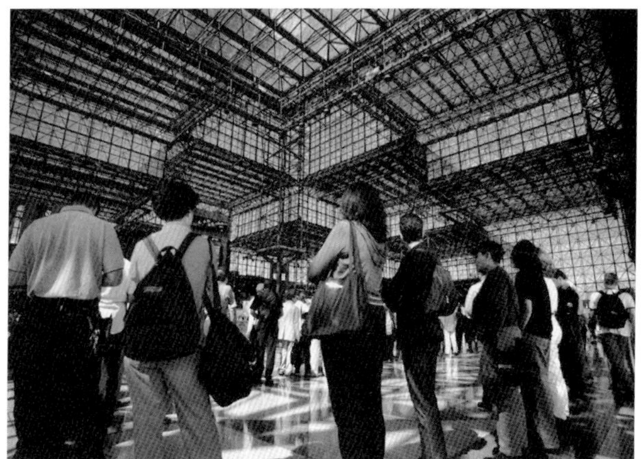

50s and above

Mary Boone Gallery

Nobody recognised more acutely than Mary Boone the point at which being located on a ground floor on West Broadway became more of a liability than an asset. Traditionally the stronghold and epicentre of the contemporary art scene, Soho has as of late been taken over by chain stores such as Starbucks (coffee), Vicoria's Secret (lingerie), and Pottery Barn (homeware). What used to be the stomping ground of major collectors and those in the art-world know, has become a roofless shopping mall for the tri-state area.

In 1993 Boone knew it was time to go. But then her timing has always been impeccable. In 1977 Boone opened her first gallery in 420 West Broadway, home to the legendary dealers Leo Castelli and Ileana Sonnabend. At only 25 years old, the pint-sized Boone was way beyond her years in business savvy. Showing the likes of Julian Schnabel and Jean Michel Basquiat, her gallery was the springboard from which massive careers were launched.

In 1981 Boone opened a larger space at 417 West Broadway. During this decade she was the epitome of the wheeling-dealing-international-art operator and has boasted everyone from Jeff Koons to Eric Fischl and Barbara Kruger in her lineup at one time or another. Soho happened, and Boone was a key factor in its success. She had an empire that could not be toppled, even after the scandalous defection of her star artist Schnabel to Pace Gallery in 1984.

Boone expanded her empire when she merged, romantically as well as professionally, with German *uber*dealer Michael Werner. Having met in 1982 at the aptly named 'Zeitgeist' exhibition in Berlin, they married four years later. Werner's army of artists, which included Georg Baselitz, A R Penck and Jorg Immendorff, combined with Boone's battalion, made them the golden couple of the art world. Boone's artists were given the

Mary Boone Gallery

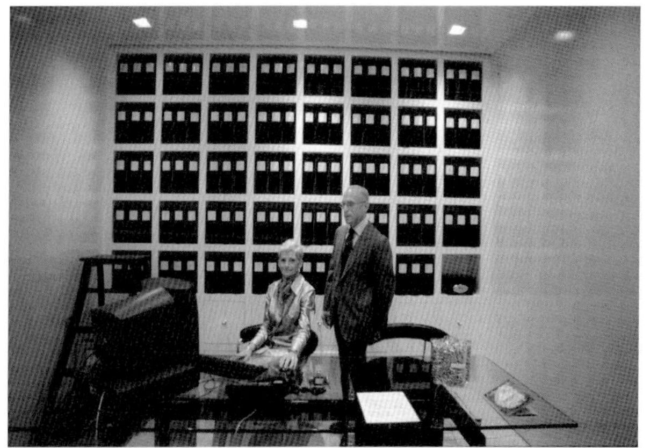

chance to show in Germany while Werner's prestigious lineup contributed to his wife's continuing rise. Boone and Werner became a fixture in society columns, mingling with the rich and glamorous.

Displaying her staunch individuality, Boone remained unique among her Soho colleagues in her decision to relocate. Ignoring the opportunities in Chelsea, she decided instead to move uptown. This move has finally placed her on the pedestal on which she belongs. Proximity to the museums (the Museum of Modern Art, the Metropolitan Museum of Art, the Whitney and the Guggenheim), as well as to Pace, Gagosian, and C&M was a motivating factor – this is where all the high-end deals take place. But unlike the galleries she wants to be seen on a financial par with, her space has kept a downtown edge in its design. Concrete floors, grey walls, and an office that looks like it belongs in the 22nd century were the designed by architect Richard Gluckman.

Despite its uptown address Mary Boone Gallery does not show only blue-chip artists. For example, Ellen Gallagher, a 29-year-old African-American artist, was snapped up by Boone; her work is now been placed in the New York MOMA, the Metropolitan Museum of Art, the Los Angeles Museum of Contemporary Art, and the Denver Art Museum. But true to her roots Boone keeps a beefy roster including Richard Artschwager, Ross Bleckner and David Salle.

ADDRESS 745 Fifth Avenue, New York, NY 10151 (212 752 2929)
HOURS Tuesday to Friday, 10.00–18.00; Saturday, 10.00-17.00
SUBWAY 59th Street N, R

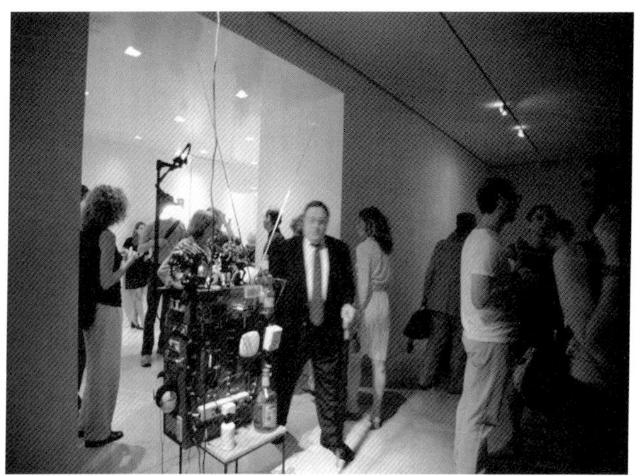

Leo Castelli Gallery

A few years ago, Leo Castelli celebrated his 90th birthday with a glamorous bash at New York's Soho Grand Hotel. Gathered among the great and the good were stars from various galaxies, including Bianca Jagger, Roy Lichtenstein and Anna Sui. They came to pay tribute to Castelli's role as the undisputed king of the post-war New York artworld. Similarly, upon his death in 1999, major column inches in all the reputable publications commemorated the life and work of this legendary art dealer.

An Italian-Jewish refugee, in 1957 he opened his gallery in his Upper East Side Home. At the time he was already over fifty, had a small collection with works by Giacometti and Pollock, and, more importantly, had a very rich wife, Ileana Sonnabend, who is a legend in her own right, and remained best friends with Castelli decades after the demise of their marriage in 1959.

In the heady days of the 1980s Castelli and Sonnabend were one of the great partnerships in the business of art. Together they discovered Jasper Johns and promoted Robert Rauschenberg, helped celebrate pop art and introduced the new movements in art to New Yorkers. Minimalism, conceptualism, performance, neo-expressionism and a post-pop hybrid of all the above were first showcased by Ileana and Leo.

For years the Castelli and Sonnabend galleries occupied separate floors of a four-storey building at 420 West Broadway. During the 1980s this became the nerve centre of the art world, with Castelli's annual turnover estimated at $20 billion at the height of the art market in the years directly preceding the stock-market crash. Jasper Johns and Roy Lichtenstein have always been the main money-earners for the gallery, and Castelli has therefore directed most of his attention to these two artists. Over the years, however, a who's who of the art world – Andy Warhol, Claes

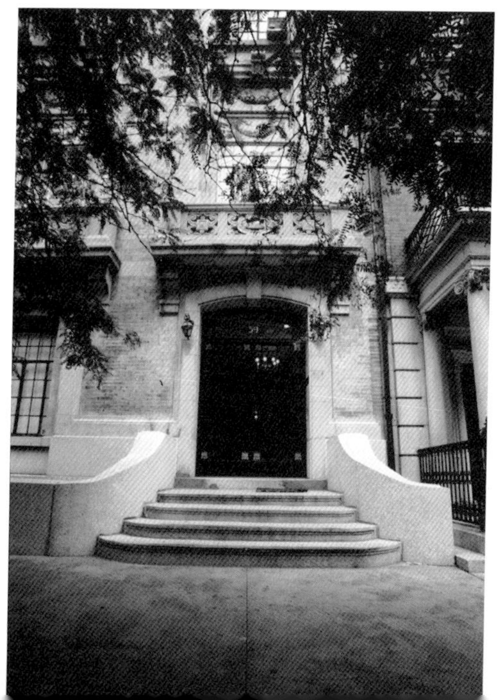

Oldenberg, Richard Serra, Donald Judd, John Chamberlain and Dan Flavin – have been represented by Castelli.

Unfortunately many of his prized artists jumped ship during the storm. Warhol died in 1987, and Claes Oldenberg left soon after. Julian Schnabel and David Salle, who were represented jointly by the Castelli and Mary Boone galleries, left for the Pace and Gagosian galleries respectively. The scrap-metal sculptor John Chamberlain and fluorescent-light sculptor Dan Flavin also left camp after feeling neglected.

However difficult it was to deal with Castelli, artists have nevertheless earned great rewards under his wing. Castelli has for over four decades been an integral part of the international art market and will remain an icon. The question is, who will ever be able to fill his shoes? Perhaps his 29-year-old widow might make a stab at it. However, the newer breed of art dealers in Manhattan is manifestly a different generation operating in a world where a fickle media allows for even fewer than fifteen minutes of fame.

ADDRESS 59 East 79th Street, New York, NY 10021 (212 249 4470)
OPEN Tuesday to Saturday, 10.00–18.00
SUBWAY 86th Street 4, 5, 6

Leo Castelli Gallery

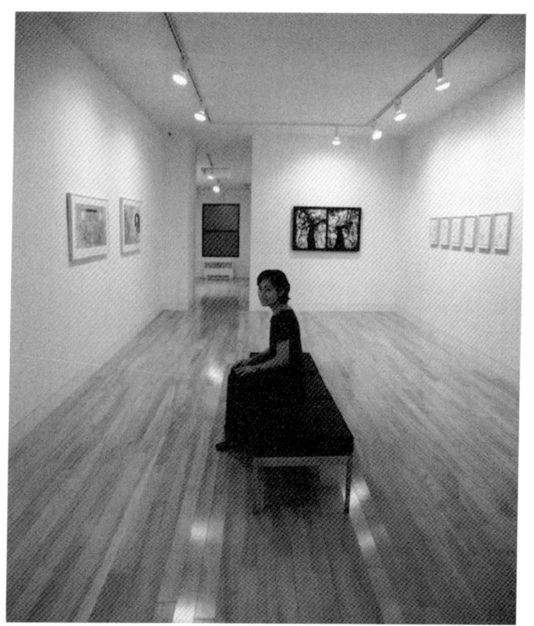

50s and above

Christie's

Christie's first ever sale took place in Pall Mall in London in 1766. Today the auctioneer's name is associated with the sale of some of the world's most expensive pieces of art, with only Sotheby's as a potential rival.

In 1977 Christie's opened its American auction house on Park Avenue. Last year a move to Rockefeller Plaza caused much excitement in the art world. The three-storey building boasts 315,000 square feet of space. Not just an auction room, it also houses impressive exhibition galleries and the offices of Christie's staff. The company has located the auction house in an architectural masterpiece. Twice the size of its former space, the new building features a soaring triple-height entranceway with a fantastically vibrant mural by Sol LeWitt. The mural continues a tradition of public art in the Rockefeller Centre, although it is the first installation since 1946. The main saleroom has dramatic double-height ceilings, able to accommodate larger work. With Christie's newest division dedicated to dealing contemporary art they will certainly need the space.

The first auction to take place in the new space was held in April 1999. 'Photographs' consisted of images spanning the history of photography from 1840 to the present. As a tribute to Rockerfeller Centre, the first lot to be auctioned was Andreas Feininger's 'Rockerfeller Center, RCA Tower' (c. 1940).

Even if you're not a potential bidder, do go along to have a look at this spectacular space and the treasures it invariably has on display.

ADDRESS 20 Rockefeller Plaza, 49th Street, New York, 10020 (212 636 2000)
HOURS Monday to Saturday, 10.00–17.00; Sunday 13.00–17.00
SUBWAY 51st Street E, F, 6

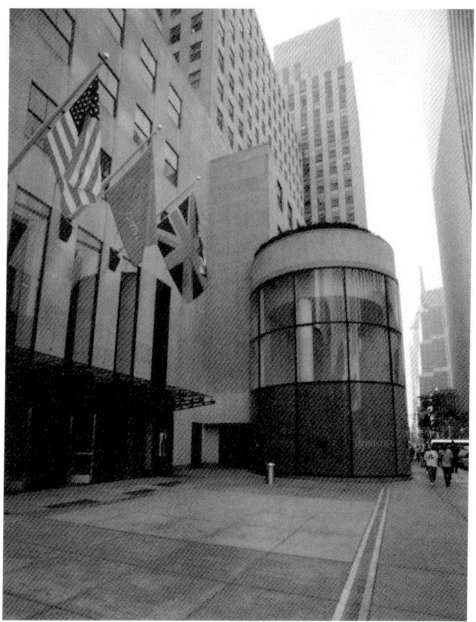

Marian Goodman Gallery

When Marian Goodman left Columbia University in the early 1960s with a degree in art history she knew that there were virtually no opportunities for a woman in the curatorial departments of museums. Not satisfied with the prospect of being a research assistant and wanting to work directly with artists, Goodman decided to start something of her own. In 1965 she founded Multiples, a venture which published prints, multiples and books by leading American artists. Working with Richard Artschwager, John Baldessari, Donald Judd, Dan Graham, Joseph Kosuth, and Andy Warhol, Goodman selected the best that American art had to offer and presented it in two-dimensional form. One of the most important achievements of Multiples was the introduction of European artists – such as Blinky Palermo, Joseph Beuys and Gerhard Richter – to an American audience.

Multiples lasted until 1975. In 1977 Goodman was ready to open her own gallery. The inagural exhibition of Marcel Broodthaers was organised before his death in 1976. Since then Goodman has built a reputation for working with the most celebrated conceptual and minimalist artists from America and abroad. Among the list, which is too long to duplicate here but is a virtual index of 'museum-worthy' artists, are such figures as Lothar Baumgarten, Anselm Kiefer, Guiseppe Penone, Thomas Struth, Jeff Wall, and Lawrence Weiner.

Dan Graham has been working with Goodman for many years. Revered for his groundbreaking work in video and performance, Graham was among the first cultural commentators of the postmodern period. Examining popular as well as high culture, Graham wrote about topics ranging from Dean Martin and The Kinks to corporate architecture. His work has been hugely influential for the younger generations of video and installation artists.

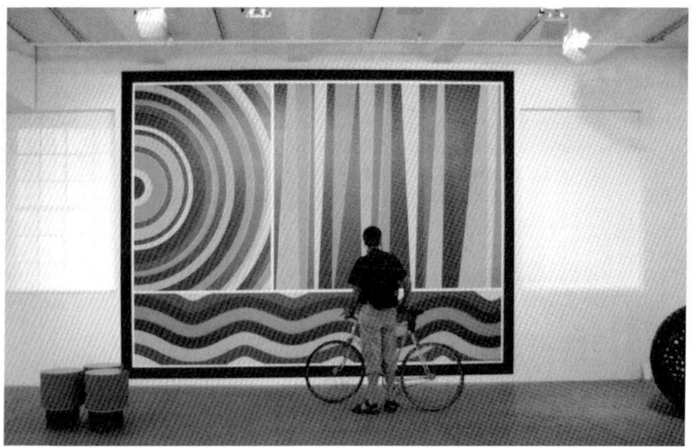

Marian Goodman Gallery

The German artist Rebecca Horn is equally celebrated. Horn began with performances in which she donned 'body extensions', filming the process in order to record the work. Later her work entailed elaborate mechanical installations that span the topics of gender, politics and romance.

Younger artists such as the Brit Steve McQueen and Mexico's Gabriel Orozco have more recently been taken under the wing of Goodman. McQueen's film-making talents were recognised when he was awarded the Turner Prize in 1999. Both of these artists are indicative of Goodman's approach to representing artists: she embraces the new at whatever age it is. Goodman's original artists – such as Graham, Weiner, and Richter – have continued to create a discourse in the gallery for more than two decades.

ADDRESS 24 West 57th Street, New York, NY 10019 (212 977 7160)
OPEN Monday to Saturday, 10.00 – 18.00
SUBWAY 59th Street N, R

Marian Goodman Gallery

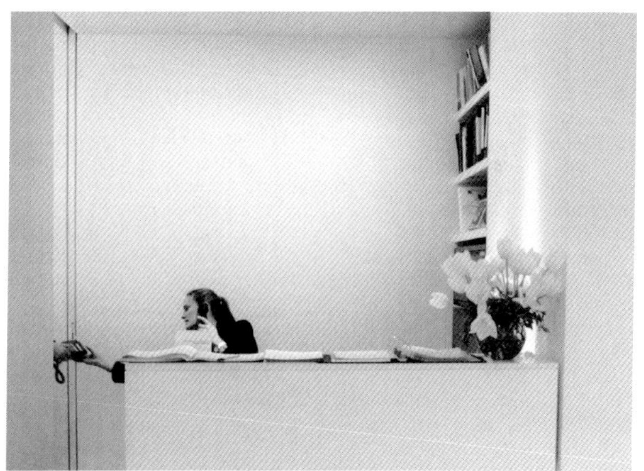

50s and above

Galerie Lelong

This is the New York headquarters of a gallery that also has spaces in Paris and Zurich. Originating in Paris, it began as a partnership between Daniel Lelong and Aime Maeght who subsequently left to start his own gallery. The Paris branch focuses on paintings and works on paper – prints, drawings and portfolios – featuring both contemporary and modern art, most by European artists. Lelong in New York focuses on contemporary photography and sculpture, and its artists all come from New York, Latin and South America. The dominant interest of the artists is the body – in landscape, as a vessel, as a site and also as an agent that registers change.

Lelong represent the estate of Ana Mendiata (her death was the subject of much controversy due to allegations that her late partner, the minimalist artist Carl Andre pushed her out of the window of their New York apartment). Mendiata made art out of leaving traces of her body, at times adorned with flowers and twigs, in the landscape. 1999 saw Galerie Lelong co-host an exhibition of Mediata's and Marina Abramovic's work with the latter's downtown dealer Sean Kelly.

Lelong also represent Andy Goldsworthy, who often sites his work in nature (and was celebrated with a show in May 2000), and Alfredo Jaar, whose work deals with the body as a register of social and historical events. Sean Scully, Waltercio Caldas and Cildo Meireles are also on Lelong's multicultural list.

ADDRESS 20 West 57th Street, New York, NY 10019 (212 315 0470)
OPEN Tuesday to Saturday, 10.00–17.30
SUBWAY 59th Street N, R

Galerie Lelong

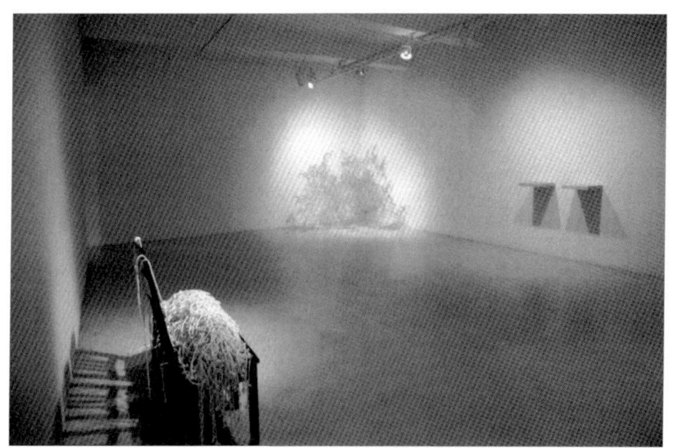

50s and above

Marlborough

Marlborough is in the same league as Leo Castelli and Gagosian, ranking as one of the most important galleries of the post-war period. It was founded in London in 1946 by Frank Lloyd and Harry Fischer, later joined by David Somerset (now the Duke of Beaufort). During the 1950s Marlborough's major shows of modern masters included Frank Auerbach, Francis Bacon, Barbara Hepworth, Henry Moore, and Graham Sutherland established it as the leading fine-art dealer in London.

By 1962 Frank Lloyd had moved to New York and opened the Midtown space, which is gargantuan in comparison to other galleries in the area. It includes an outdoor terrace which greatly enhances the shows of Marlborough sculptors such as Anthony Caro and Jacques Lipschitz.

In 1997 Marlborough joined the flock and headed south to Chelsea, where they opened a 4000-square-foot gallery at 211 West 19th Street. International Public Art, Ltd – Marlborough's independent corporation committed to the development of international public art projects with an emphasis on the integration of art, architecture, and the urban and natural environments – operates from the Chelsea site.

Like its galleries, which now operate in major cities around the world, Marlborough's roster of artists is extensive. The most prominent personalities seem chosen to fill the expansive spaces: Red Grooms, Alex Katz, Larry Rivers, R B Kitaj, and Paula Rego.

ADDRESS 40 West 57th Street, New York, NY 10019 (212 541 4900)
WEBSITE www.marlboroughgallery.com
OPEN Monday to Saturday, 10.00-17.30
SUBWAY 59th Street N, R

Marlborough

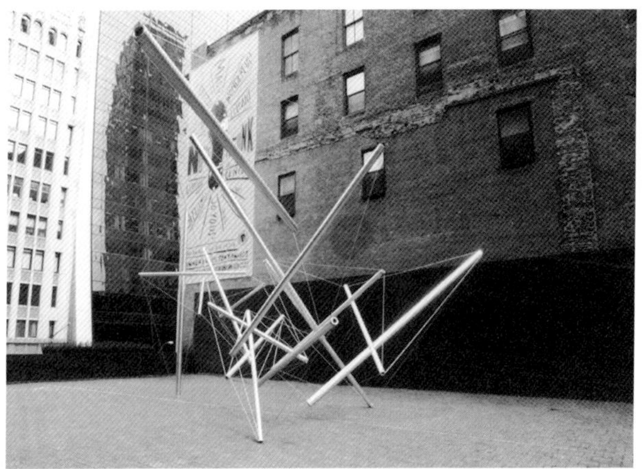

McKee

A youthful David McKee arrived in New York, fresh off the Queen Mary, in 1964. Having met many young Americans studying abroad, McKee was excited by their ideas and desperate to see the Guggenheim, Whitney, and Metropolitan Museums for himself. His first position was at the legendary Marlborough Gallery (see page 6.18) which McKee maintains is the greatest gallery in the world in regard to the range of art shown. It was there that he met his wife and current partner in the gallery, René.

McKee opened his first gallery in a converted beauty salon on 63rd Street in 1974. The gallery moved to its present location – across the hall from Mary Boone (see page 6.2) – ten years ago. McKee represents 12 artists including Daisy Youngblood and Vija Celmins. A personal love of sculpture means that his gallery has a strong identification with this art form.

McKee found America to be the perfect location for his gallery. As a Brit he is aware that here his vision has found an audience – at least as far as the number, wealth and diverse demands of collectors are concerned – that does not exist in the United Kingdom. McKee's gallery is important for its refusal to follow fashion and for its belief in independent thought.

ADDRESS 4th floor, 745 Fifth Avenue,New York, NY 10151 (212 688 5951/mckeegall@aol.com)
OPEN Tuesday to Saturday, 10.00–18.00
SUBWAY 59th Street N, R

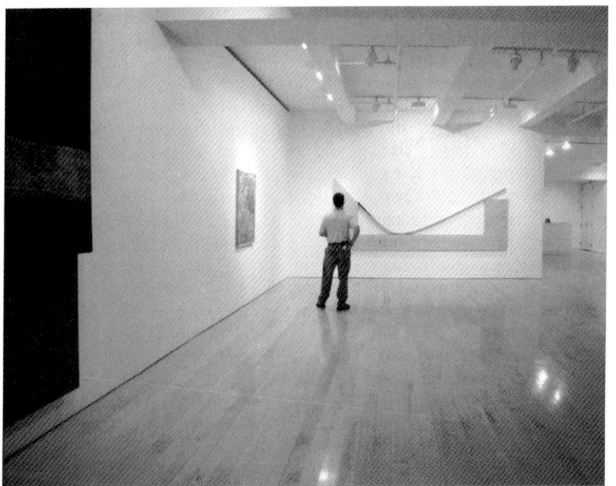

Projects at The Museum of Modern Art

6.22

New York's Museum of Modern Art contains countless masterpieces of modern and twentieth-century art, work from the days of Picasso and Cézanne to Roy Lichtenstein and Cindy Sherman. In addition to the impressive permanent collection and major exhibitions there is one room in particular which represents the cutting edge of international contemporary art. Located on the ground floor, just past the reception area and adjacent to the fantastic sculpture garden, is the space where MOMA's projects are presented.

The Project series is overseen by Robert Storr, the curator responsible for such memorable shows as Robert Ryman's retrospective and the recent retrospective of Chuck Close. Each show in the series presents the work of one artist, who is not exactly emerging, but recognised as making important contributions to the discourse of contemporary art and culture. The Projects – and several are presented each year – are shown for a short period, from a few weeks to one or two months.

Storr has presented work that is consistently intelligent and of high quality. In 1995 the Projects room hosted an installation by Ann Hamilton, who subsequently represented the United States with a stunning installation in the 1999 Venice Biennale. For Maurizio Cattelan's project in autumn 1998 the artist hired an actor dressed as a caricature version of Pablo Picasso, with the standard white and navy striped sweater and a giant head with trademark bulging brown eyes. This cartoon-like spoof of an icon of modernism greeted viewers entering the museum. The amusement-park-like tactics of Cattelan touch upon the widely held view that museums like MOMA, which present blockbuster shows of artists from the canon, are increasingly becoming satellites of the entertainment industry. How many times have you been to a blockbuster show and had to fight through crowds to see the work? It is this

Projects at The Museum of Modern Art

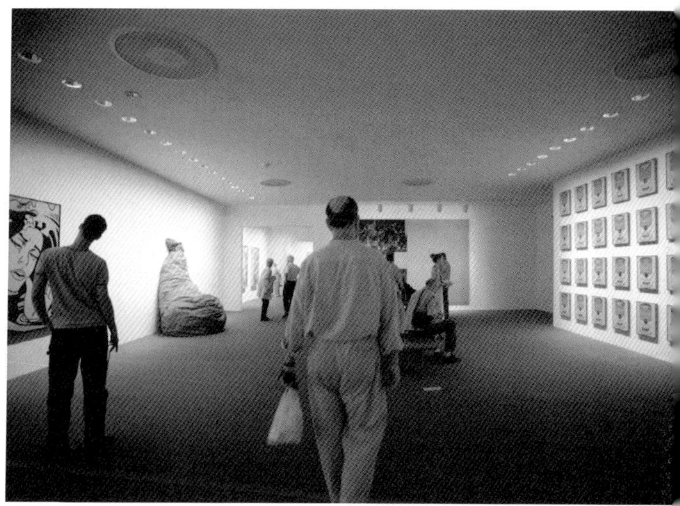

kind of attitude – so eloquently illustrated by Cattelan – that makes the Projects series special. It gives younger and less-established artists the opportunity to express their views, even if they are critical of the institutions that support their work.

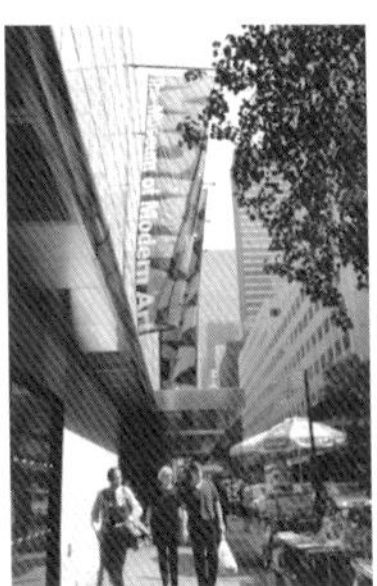

ADDRESS 11 West 53rd Street, New York, NY 10019 (212 708 9480)
WEBSITE www.moma.org
OPEN Saturday to Tuesday, Thursday, 10.30–17.45; Friday, 10.30–20.15
SUBWAY 53rd Street E, F

Projects at The Museum of Modern Art

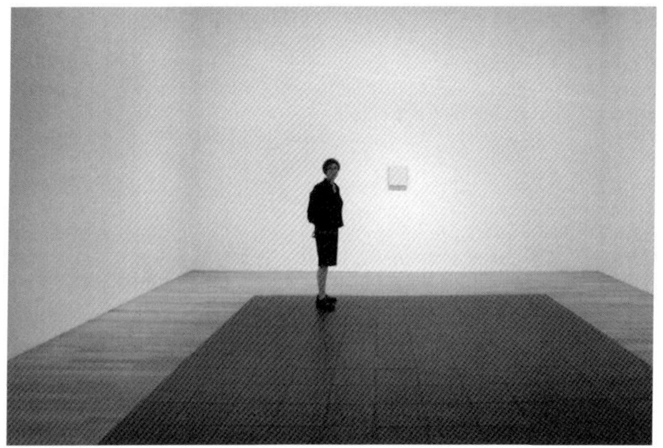

50s and above

PaceWildenstein

Impressive is an understatement for the list of artists on PaceWildenstein's roster. Among 32 glitterati of the art world are Chuck Close, George Condo, Claes Oldenburg and Coosje van Bruggen, Robert Ryman, Kiki Smith, and Joel Shapiro. The gallery represents the estates of such luminaries as Alexander Calder, Pablo Picasso and Mark Rothko, as well as dealing with works by the late Donald Judd, Dan Flavin and Henry Moore.

Spread over a number of floors in a multi-storey building on 57th Street, the gallery actually comprises three galleries under the PaceWildenstein banner. On entering the lowest level a visitor finds the PaceWildenstein gallery, which features exhibitions by its own artists. Above this is PaceWildensteinMacGill, which specialises in photography under the supervision of leading photography dealer Peter MacGill. Higher up is Pace Prints, Pace Primitive and Pace Master Prints. These factions give the gallery a corporate feel, and PaceWildenstein is now considered a very establishment institution.

PaceWildenstein as it is known today has only existed since 1993. Founded as the Pace Gallery in Boston, Massachusetts, in 1960, it moved to New York three years later and grew steadily over the next two decades. By the early 1980s Pace had proven itself to be a major player in the world of modern and contemporary dealing. By 1990 Pace needed to expand its space in order to accommodate a growing variety and number of artists. The solution came in the form of a new exhibition space at 142 Greene Street in Soho.

In 1993 Pace merged with Wildenstein & Co, who had the world's largest private inventory of impressionist works and old masters. The amalgamation was successful and has seen the operation spread even further afield to yet another exhibition space on Wilshire Boulevard in

PaceWildenstein

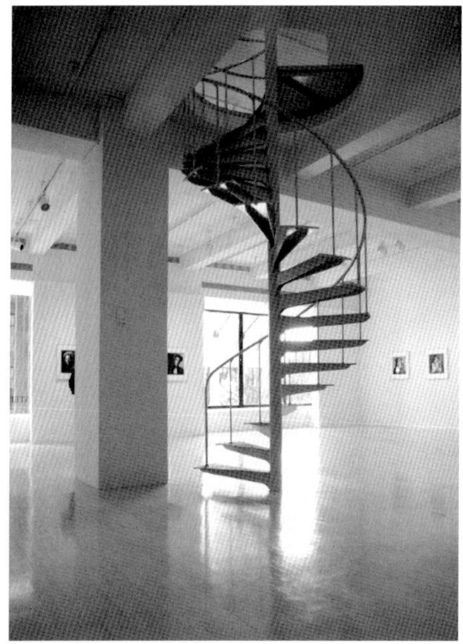

50s and above

Beverly Hills. This merger has brought much publicity to the gallery during the past few years, and some of it has been rather unsavoury. The Wildenstein family, who are long-established collectors steeped in New York society, have borne the brunt of speculation about the origins of some of the art found in their collection. In addition, the unlucky marriage of David and Joyce Wildenstein recently dissolved amid rumours and accusations of violence. The press had a field day – even *Vanity Fair* saw fit to run a full-length feature on the troubled family.

Despite all the adverse attention, PaceWildenstein continue to play a more than significant role in the twentieth-century secondary market. The gallery's ultra-professional attitude will certainly engender confidence in elite international collectors. However, this is not the place to visit if it is new ideas and experimentation you are seeking.

ADDRESS 32 East 57th Street, New York, NY 10022 (212 421 3292)
WEBSITE www.pacewildenstein.com
OPEN Tuesday to Friday, 9.30–17.30; Saturday, 10.00–18.00
SUBWAY 59th Street, N, R

PaceWildenstein

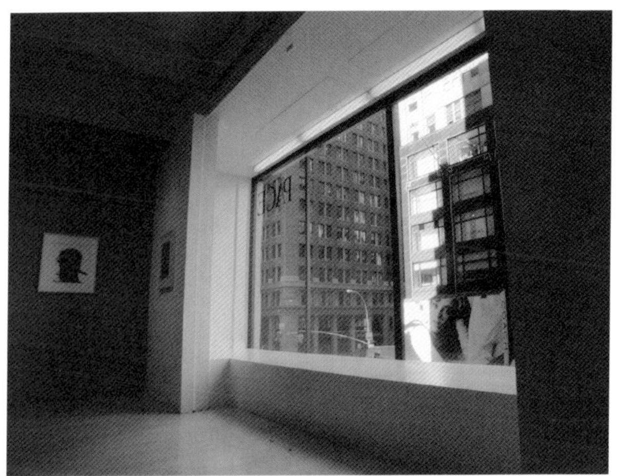

50s and above

Saks Fifth Avenue Collection and Saks Project Art

Saks Fifth Avenue, the department store that boasts the Plaza Hotel and Trump Tower as neighbours, is host to an intriguing programme of contemporary art. The project has two elements: a permanent collection hung throughout the store, and Saks Fifth Avenue Project Art, temporary exhibitions curated in the windows. Mary Dinaburg, curator and driving force behind the Saks collection, brings art to a wide audience: more than 20,000 people walk by the windows daily and thousands venture inside.

The rationale behind the project is economic, a marketing strategy that is meant to impress customers. Two years ago Ken Smart, vice president of corporate visual presentation at Saks Fifth Avenue, realised that an a lot of money was being spent on art that was essentially decorative with no resale value. Dinaburg was hired to select works by emerging artists, and naturally this work is expected to increase in value over time. For example, the investment value of a series of prints by Chris Ofili has been boosted by his winning of the 1998 Turner Prize. As well as pleasing customers and enhancing the working lives of staff, the purchasing policy supports an intricate system of young artists and dealers.

Works acquired by Saks are placed permanently in various departments with plaques noting title, artist's name, and media. For example, several small David Craven paintings are subtly placed in the Missoni section. Craven's paintings, featuring discordant fields of colour, protrusions, words and symbols, cohabit well with Missoni's multi-coloured and patterned knitwear. However, even if fashion designs change, the paintings remain where they have been placed. Thus the art is chosen to integrate with the architecture more than the designs on the shop floor.

While it might be argued that corporate sponsors are necessarily limited in terms of the content of the art they present, a recent Saks Fifth

Saks Fifth Avenue Collection and Saks Project Art

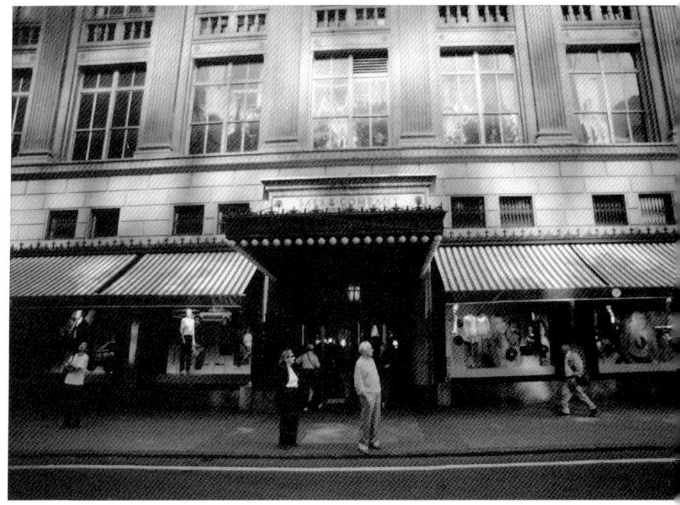

Avenue Project Art was concerned with difficult social issues. Exhibited in the store's windows, *Fever: The Art of David Wojnarowicz* contained works that reflected this prolific artist's crusade against homophobia in relation to AIDS. Considering that the windows are located directly next to St Patrick's Cathedral, the ideological home of Catholicism in New York, one might have expected some kind of outcry. No-one complained.

Placing art in shops guarantees an audience, while the challenge is to retain their attention. While the Saks project has at its root a commercial motive, it nevertheless encourages young artists and provokes discourse. It attempts to interweave various disciplines in order to heighten awareness of contemporary culture. For example, a recent exhibition invited ten famous designers to make clothes inspired by Sigmund Freud. These garments were exhibited in the windows next to work made by artists who have been influenced by the great psychoanalyst. In May 1999 an exhibition featured seminal work by Vito Acconci, the famous video and conceptual artist.

The Saks programme proves that corporations can do much to support the work of emerging and more-established artists. The programme takes art out of the museum and into the streets and the shopping mall. It proves that the days of a clear-cut definition of public art have passed – gone is the notion of monumental sculpture placed in a piazza. Challenging art can be found anywhere—even in the middle of a shopping centre.

ADDRESS 611 5th Avenue, New York, NY 10017 (212 753 4000)
OPEN Mondayto Saturday, 10.00–19.00; Sunday, 12.00–18.00
SUBWAY 51st Street 6, E, F

Saks Fifth Avenue Collection and Saks Project Art

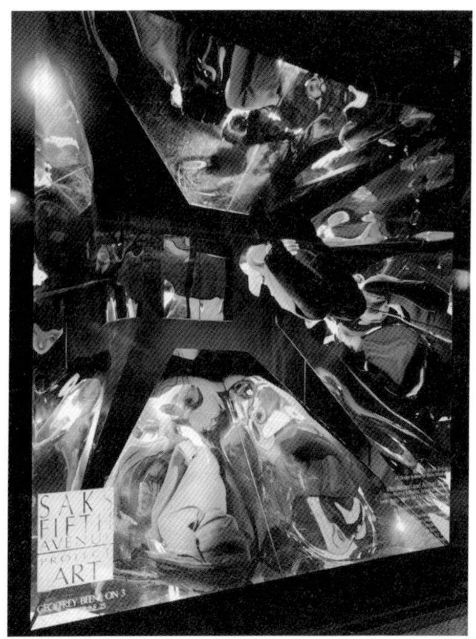

Ubu Gallery

Père Ubu was the surreal invention of the French writer Alfred Jarry in 1896. Ubu as a gallery reflects this idea in full: a proto-surrealist name evoking the surrealist work presented. And – like the surrealist movement – all the artists represented are dead.

Ubu Gallery is the cumulative effort of three New Yorkers: Jack Banning, Adam Boxer and Rosa Esman. Esman had had her own gallery for 20 years, opening on 80th Street in the mid 1970s and closing in Soho in 1993, when the commercialism of the area became overwhelming. It was time to move uptown.

Jack Banning, former owner of Poster America, had collaborated with Esman on an exhibition of Russian Revolutionary posters, books and drawings. The two approached the third partner, Adam Boxer, who was dealing in Surrealist photography and had worked with Banning on exhibitions at Poster America. The three were bound by a shared interest in modernism and Ubu was born at its current address in 1994.

Virtually hidden on the ground level of tree-lined 78th Street, the gallery was curiously, already celebrated before Esman, Banning and Boxer moved in. In a previous incarnation it had been the locus of Bianchini Gallery, which launched the high-profile exhibition, *The Great American Pop Store,* in 1964.

These days collectors seek to be on the mailing list of Ubu Gallery as their invitations – all designed by Adam's wife, Eileen Boxer – are themselves virtually collector's items. For example, for Richard Tipping's *Perversions, Subversions and Verse*, Ubu sent out mini bicycle license plates, replacing the Statue of Liberty (found on all NY vehicle license plates) with the figure of Ubu. For the 1999 exhibition of Hans Bellmer's photographs and drawings from the 1930s, Ubu reproduced handpainted photographs of Bellmer's dolls enclosed within an ecru folder tied with

Ubu Gallery

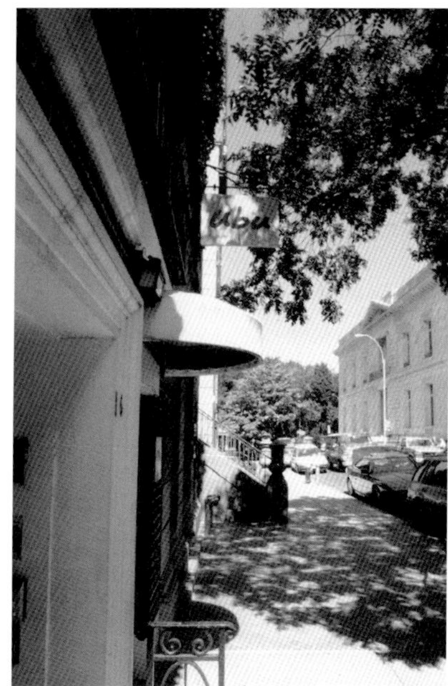

a black ribbon. For a Rodchenko show, the gallery fabricated a badge recreating the artist's design of an airplane bearing the name of Ubu.

So Ubu Gallery does not simply create exhibitions. The partners use the space for stimulating group shows based on modernist themes. *The 60s in the 70s* – an exhibition referring to the 1960s in the streets of the East Seventies – paid homage to the neighbourhood galleries in the heady times of pop, conceptual and performance art.

The gallery also attracts wide media attention. An exhibition entitled *One-Line Drawing* was videotaped and presented on ABC *News* many times over the summer of 1997. An exhibition of Yoko Ono's work, *Drawings from Franklin Summer and Blood Objects from Family Albums*, re-introduced early instruction works, presented recent cast sculpture and new pointillist drawings. The exhibition attracted an enormous number of viewers and journalistic attention.

Not that Ubu appear to need it; between its desirable invitations and the edgy shows it mounts, Ubu has become an uptown meeting place for the cognoscenti.

ADDRESS 16 East 78th Street, New York, NY 10021 (212 794 4444)
OPEN Tuesday to Saturday, 11.00–18.00
SUBWAY 77th Street 6

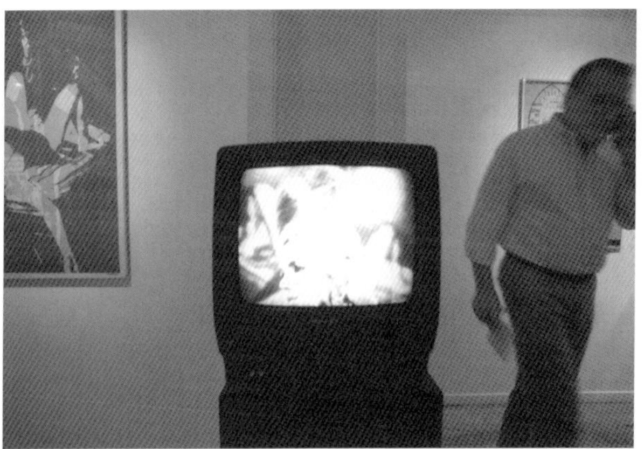

Kaufman Astoria Studios Film and Video Gallery

The Whitney has New York's longest-running museum programme devoted to avant-garde film and video. Established in 1970, the Film and Video Department is dedicated to the presentation of avant-garde and experimental film, single-channel videotapes, and film and video installations by film-makers and artists. The Kaufman Astoria Studios Film and Video Gallery is a project space located in the second floor galleries at the Whitney Museum of American Art. It is a 30 x 40-foot space with a high ceiling. The space is flexible, moving between a white cube showing installations by artists, to a black box showing new and historical avant-garde and underground film.

In addition to curating large shows on the main floors, Chrissie Iles is the curator of the Film and Video Gallery. A specialist in film and video installation, Iles made her name as curator at The Museum of Modern Art in Oxford, England. Here she organised such illustrious shows as *Scream* and *Scream Again*. In 1998 Iles crossed the Atlantic to take up her position at the Whitney – another Brit who is making a mark in New York's art world. Her focus is on the ways film and art relate to each other, shown clearly in the popularity of film for artists such as Stan Douglas, Shirin Neshat, Gary Hill, Douglas Gordon and Matthew Barney. Iles is keen to tap into New York's young film world. Her aim is to create an exciting interdisciplinary dialogue between film-makers and artists.

One of the feats that Iles has already performed is to establish a new acquisitions committee for film and performance tapes as well as documentation at the Whitney. Iles is actively collating videos of American performance art, which she believes must be integrated into the Whitney's collection. Casting her net wide, Iles has reeled in some obscure and amusing works by Richard Serra (featuring the hand of Philip Glass

Kaufman Astoria Studios Film and Video Gallery

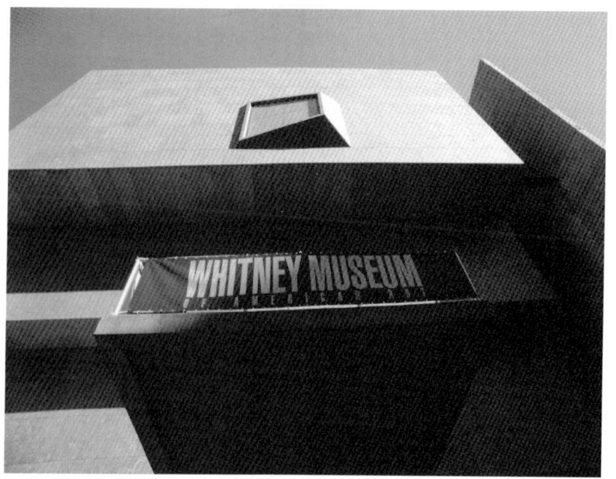

opening and closing in an attempt to catch falling objects), Joan Jonas ('Songdelay' was shot in 1975 in the wasteland that is now the gleaming Battery Park City), Paul McCarthy, Vito Acconci and Robert Morris.

A number of special collections are also being formed, including Castelli-Sonnabend Tapes and Films, an archive of films and video by artists that include Bruce Nauman, Dennis Oppenheim, Ed Ruscha, and Robert Smithson, which are being reassembled for the first time since their original production in the early 1970s. Since the 1980s, in collaboration with the MOMA, the Whitney's Film and Video Department has spearheaded a major inter-museum project which catalogues, researches, preserves and re-releases the films of Andy Warhol.

Film and video works have always been important components of The Whitney's prestigious *Biennial* exhibitions. Always a well-debated (and well-attended), event, since 1932 the exhibition has presented vanguard developments in contemporary art; in fact many of today's most recognised artists have made their museum debuts in a Whitney Biennial.

Most of the Whitney's 1999 programme was dedicated to a two-part exhibition, *The American Century: Art and Culture 1900–2000*. The accompanying film series included more than 200 films, shown in their entirety in the Kaufmann Astoria Studios Film and Video Gallery. In Part Two Iles invited film curator Mark Webber –from the British band Pulp – to select a programme of American underground films from the 1960s. Webber has also been invited to guest curate 1960s American underground film at the Whitney on a regular basis. Young New York film curators Brian Frye, Bradley Eros and Mark McElhatten have been enlisted to curate an ongoing series of expanded cinema events, both historical and contemporary, at the Whitney.

The Whitney's millennial line-up is ambitious. After the *Biennial*,

Kaufman Astoria Studios Film and Video Gallery

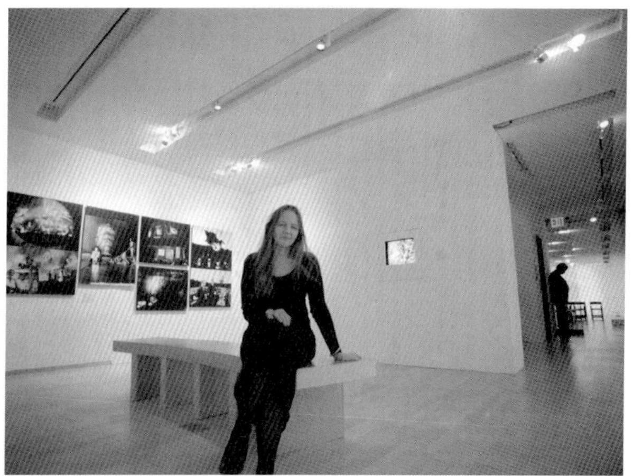

which ran until June, retrospectives of Alice Neel, Barbara Kruger and Sol LeWitt were planned for the summer and autumn respectively. To accompany the Alice Neel and Barbara Kruger shows, Iles presented a survey of women avant-garde film-makers from the 1930s to the present, followed by a survey of the 1960s psychedelic film-maker Jud Yalkut. In spring 2001 the film and video department will take over the main galleries with a show of *Film and Video Installation in America 1965–1975*. The first of its kind, it will combine film and video, reconstructing key early works by artists including Dan Graham, Vito Acconci, Dennis Oppenheim, Robert Morris and Bruce Nauman. Celebrating the work of these important figures from the 1960s, the exhibition will also spotlight the important contributions of the film and video department.

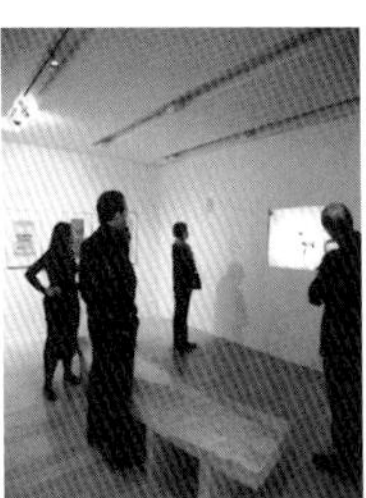

ADDRESS 945 Madison Avenue at 75th Street, New York, NY 10021 (212 570-3676 for film and video information)
WEBSITE www.whitney.org
OPEN Wednesday, 11.00–18.00; Thursday, 13.00–20.00; Friday to Sunday, 11.00–18.00
SUBWAY 77th Street at Lexington Avenue 6

Kaufman Astoria Studios Film and Video Gallery

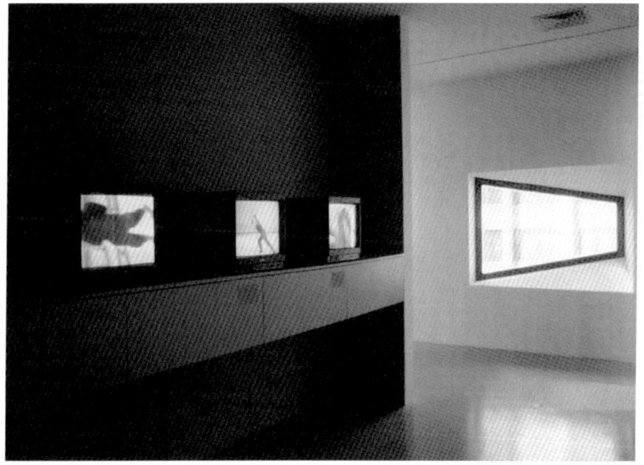

harlem

The Project 7.2

The Project

Far from the madding crowds of Soho and Chelsea, the cavernous space (all 10,000 square feet of it!) of The Project is spread over three floors in an abandoned nightclub in Harlem. Alongside its earlier incarnation as the Body Shop disco, the building had been used as an auto-repair shop.

Christian Haye, previously a writer for *frieze* magazine, opened this alternative gallery space in 1998 when he was just 29 years old. He chose Harlem so that people would come specifically to see what was showing rather than visiting a myriad of shows in the shopping mall of Chelsea. The historical significance of Harlem was a selling point for Haye, who believes it to be the most historically elegant neighbourhood in Manhattan. He is aware that being off the beaten path also allows him more room for experimentation.

The Project's inaugural show brought together 24 of Haye's favourite artists, such as Marina Abramovic, Nari Ward, Kim Dingle, Juan Muñoz, Nader, Olafur Eliasson and Soo Ja Kim. The success of the show brought some of these artists under his wing. Also in his stable are Maria Elena Gonzalez, Daniel J Martinex and Tom Gidley, Haye's former editor at *frieze*.

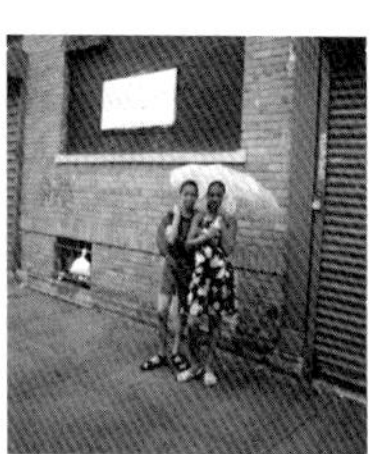

ADDRESS 416 West 126th Street, New York (212 662 8610)
WEBSITE www.elproyecto.com
HOURS Thursday to Saturday, 12.00–18.00
SUBWAT West 125th Street A, B, C, D

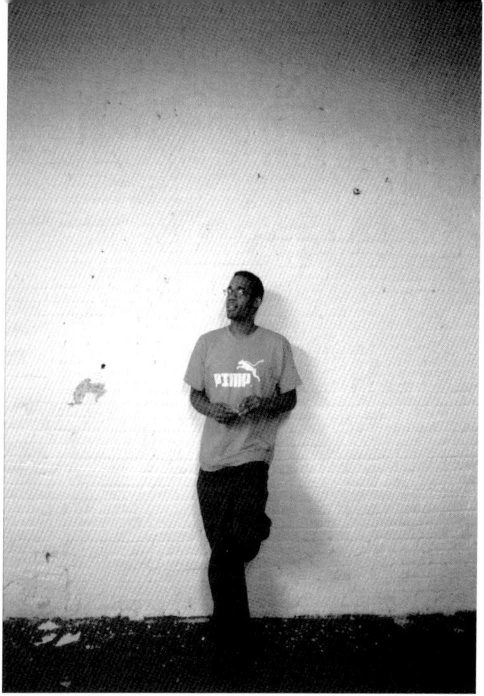

brooklyn

Art in the Anchorage

Presenting public art projects all over New York City for the past 28 years, Creative Time is a non-profit art foundation whose endeavours are just as likely to be seen scrawled in laser on a building in the Lower East Side as they are walking down a runway that has been erected in Times Square for one day during fashion week. Their projects are not usually site specific and they encourage their artists to approach New York City as their landscape and laboratory.

For the past 17 years Creative Time has been programming the space inside the anchorage of the Brooklyn Bridge. Three storeys high and built from huge blocks of granite, this space is only used in the summer months as during the rest of the year it remains unheated and unbearably cold. Art in the Anchorage, as it has been coined, was born in 1983 – the year of the Brooklyn Bridge's centennial – and four years ago Creative Time began what has become a very popular programme now known as Music in the Anchorage, which even includes the odd all-night rave. With acoustics to rival Grand Central Station, on occasion another magnificent public concert hall, DJs such as Spooky, Olive and Soulslinger have been known to use all eight chambers of the Anchorage.

Creative Time has utilised other unexpected areas of the city to play host to contemporary art. In 1993 the 42nd Street Art Project placed the works of Karen Finley, Todd Oldham and Diller and Scofidio in shopfronts on this notorious strip – now taken over by Disney and gentrified, Creative Time had a presence before the megastores moved in. Shimon Attie's project, 'Between Dreams and History', grew out of the experiences of people living on the lower east side of Manhattan. Attie interviewed the residents around Ludlow Street, extracting their most poignant ideas and dreams, which were programmed by computer and

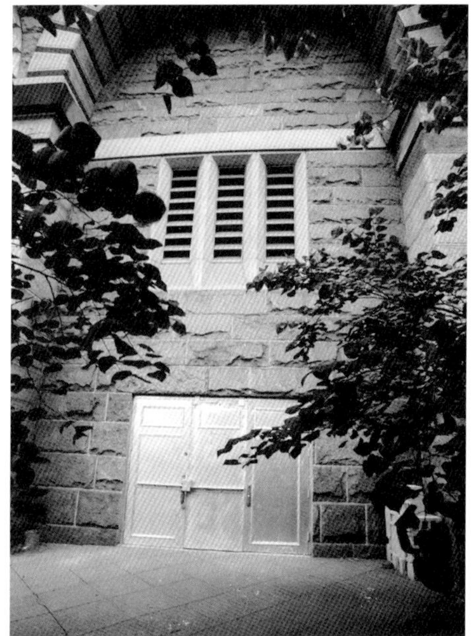

projected via laser, as if they were being written and unwritten, on to the façades of buildings in the neighbourhood.

The list of artists whose imaginations have been tapped by Creative Time over the past three decades reads as a virtual 'Who's Who' of the arts and includes such talent as Laurie Anderson, Red Grooms, Jenny Holzer, Robert Wilson and Nam June Paik. Due to its unique approach to site specification – essentially it doesn't have one – Creative Time remains at the forefront of art that is both interactive and ephemeral.

ADDRESS 1 Cadman Plaza West (212 206 6674)
WEBSITE www.creativetime.org
OPEN visit website for information on forthcoming events

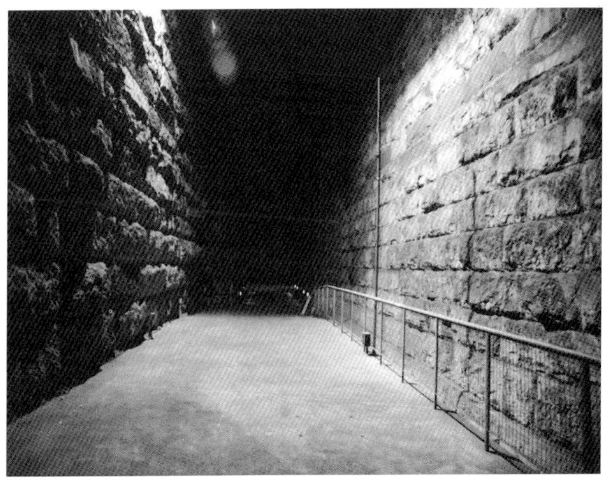

eyewash

It would be easy to miss eyewash if you didn't know it was there. Located in a domestic space on North 7th Street in Williamsburg, a tiny unassuming sign is the only indication that a gallery exists in the building. While there has been a boom in property prices and rentals (and the density of galleries) in this area of Brooklyn, the block that is home to eyewash is testimony to Williamsburg's less glamorous past. Just across the street from the gallery are industrial buildings, a garage, and tract-style housing. Yet, ironically, it is situated at the nerve centre of artistic activity in Williamsburg.

Eyewash is the brainchild of artists Larry Walczak and Anne Herron. The space is funded by Walczak, who also lives and has a studio upstairs from the gallery. Herron was previously director of Test Site; another Williamsburg-based commercial gallery that was funded by a private backer. Eyewash is a two-person operation, with Walczak and Herron being solely responsible for selecting the artists, hanging the work and publicising events.

The gallery is located on the third and sometimes fourth floors of the building. It had remained empty for 20 years due to a landlady who did not want to rent the apartment. Walczak convinced her to let them use the space in return for general upkeep and frequent paint jobs; a small price to pay for a space that could be rented for at least $1500 per month. Typically domestic elements add to the character of this apartment turned gallery: ten-and -a-half-foot ceilings, an abundance of natural light and stripped wooden floors.

Thus far the gallery has hosted only group shows. The artists are mostly based locally; however eyewash has shown work from throughout the United States. Every two or three months they curate an exhibition which occupies both the gallery and Walczak's studio space. One such exhibition

eyewash

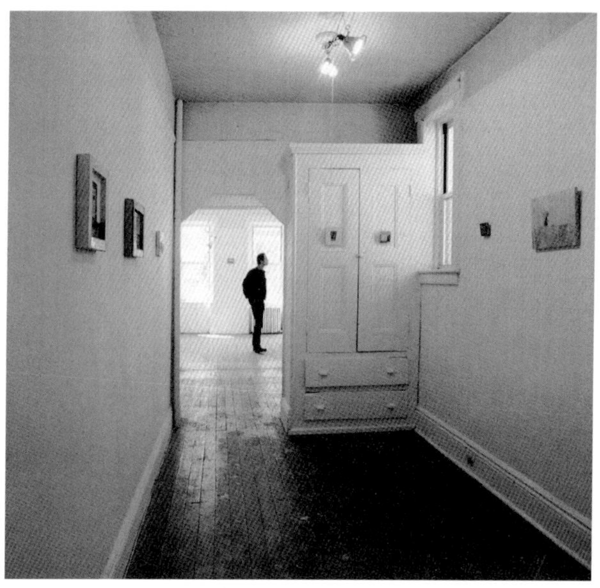

brooklyn

was 1999's Valentine's show which included a piece by Walczak who had placed an advert in the singles column of the *Village Voice* and broadcast the vocal responses of hopeful applicants on a looped answer-machine tape.

At eyewash artists are invited to install work that is adaptable to this essentially domestic space. China cabinets, sinks, toilets and bathtubs are the backdrop for the work. Eyewash took this point to its natural conclusion in 1999 with *Apartment Living*, a group show where artists were invited to take a room and respond to this theme by installing specially designed pieces directly on/into the shelves, doors, bathtub and other permanent fixtures that make up the duplex.

ADDRESS 143 North 7th Street, Williamsburg, NY 11211 (718 387 2714)
OPEN Saturday and Sunday, 13.00–18.00
SUBWAY Bedford Avenue L

eyewash

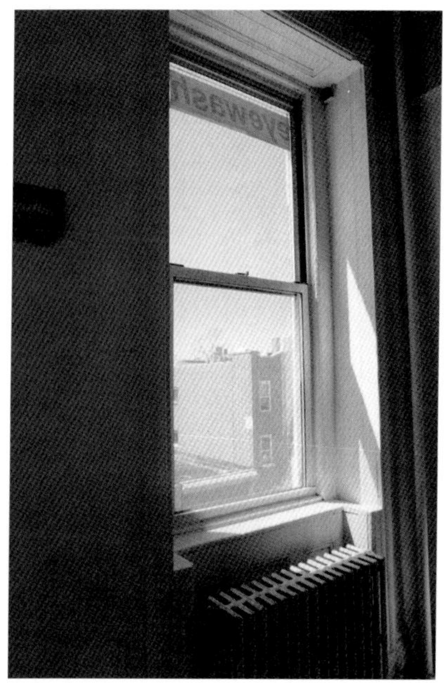

brooklyn

Feed

Worth visiting more for the space itself than what might be found in it, Feed is one of the newest galleries to open in Williamsburg. Run by the amiable couple Barry Hylton and Lisa Schroeder, the gallery is adjacent to their living quarters. Ironically, they often open the hallway that links the two parts of their lives as additional exhibition space. But do not think that this is simply a studio tacked on to the side of a gallery. Feed as an architectural entity is massive with one exposed wall that opens via sliding industrial doors. Hylton and Schroeder are only too aware of the financial potential of Feed. They rent it out as a commercial space for fashion shoots and it has already been used as the set of a feature film.

Located on the second floor, the space is both glamorous and amazing (it leaves visitors longing to move into loft-style apartments in Brooklyn) – unfortunately, the art shown thus far does not live up to its surroundings.

ADDRESS 173A North 3rd Street, Brooklyn, NY 11211 (718 486 8992)
OPEN Saturday and Sunday, 13.00–18.00
SUBWAY Bedford Avenue L

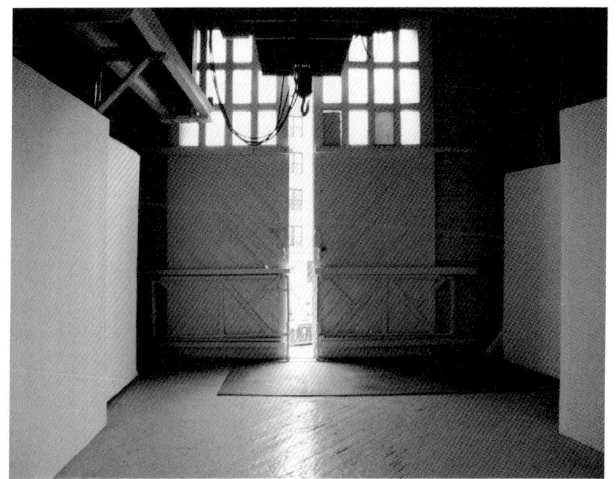

momenta art

One of the new artist-run spaces springing up in the creative hotbed of Williamsburg, in the same vicinity as eyewash and Pierogi 2000, momenta art was established in Philadelphia in 1986 by Eric Heist. Its mission was to show emerging artists who had been ignored by larger galleries. In 1993 Heist moved to New York and organised roving exhibitions. In 1994 momenta art opened in Brooklyn under the guidance of Heist and Laura Parnes, both artists. Their intention is to show complex, conceptual work that is not necessarily object-oriented. Normally they host two one-person exhibitions at the same time. They tend to show almost exclusively American artists (most of them from New York).

Momenta also hosts the occasional group show, including the 1999 exhibition *Nobodies Home*. This was concerned with living space and alienation and included a wide range of artists, from Betty Beaumont to the Brooklyn Architects Collective to the legendary Dan Graham. Yet its most effective piece was that stuck out on the façade. A *trompe l'oeil* painting suggested a 1970s-styled housewife peering out of faux doors.

Inside, the gallery is essentially a domestic space consisting of two small rooms with little natural light. Although not very impressive in scale, momenta art holds its own in concept and programme.

This is not a commercial venture and much of momenta's success relies on funding. Studios behind momenta are also administered by the gallery. These are offered at a rate less than usual for the neighbourhood, giving local artists a much-needed break, and emphasising momenta's dedication to the community rather than the commercial world.

ADDRESS 72 Berry Street, Brooklyn, NY 11211 (718 218 8058)
OPEN Friday to Monday, 12.00–18.00
SUBWAY Bedford Avenue L

momenta art

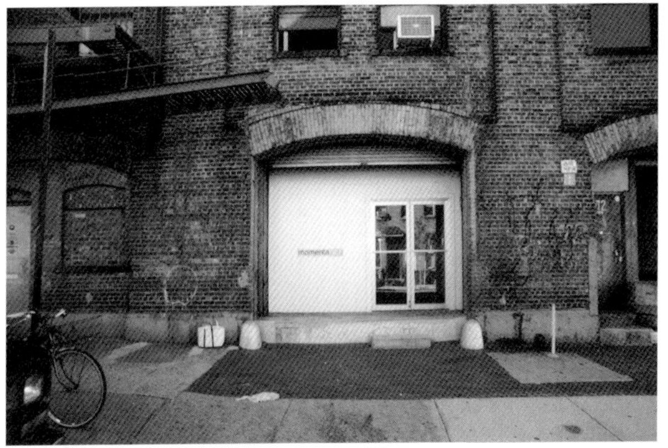

Pierogi 2000

Pierogi is a Polish dumpling – a dish prevalent in this predominantly Polish area, and the fare that director Joe Amrhein serves with cold vodka at his openings. Amrhein, who is an artist, moved to New York from California ten years ago. Frustrated with the lack of space dedicated to showing emerging artists, in September 1994 he started a gallery in his studio next door to the current location.

Pierogi 2000 opened in February 1999 with *Rage for Art*, a group show featuring artists whom Amrhein had shown individually over the previous four years. As it is an artist-run space, Amrhein is able to show artists such as Peter Garfield, Dan Devine, and Bob & Roberta Smith, although he does not actually represent them.

In addition to the gallery's exhibition programme, Amrhein has organised files featuring samples of work from more than 400 (mostly but not exclusively American) artists. These files, which began with a mere 20 artists, are available for anyone to see, as long as the compulsory white gloves are donned while viewing the original work that is for sale. Amrhein came up with this idea in an effort to make affordable work available to everyone. Each file has eight to ten pieces by an artist, with most of the work on paper, and featuring a few sculptures.

Impressive names, including Lawrence Weiner and Peter Garfield, feature on the list of artists and international dealers and curators are now aware of the incredible range of work to be found in these files. Pierogi 2000 has become a node on every collectors' itinerary.

The files have travelled to London and Venice and Amrhein is active in seeing them move further afield in order to provide exposure for the artists and to open up opportunities for people with less money to begin collecting art. As a result of this Amrhein remains in a uniquely neutral position as neither dealer nor artist. He makes a point of maintaining his

Pierogi 2000

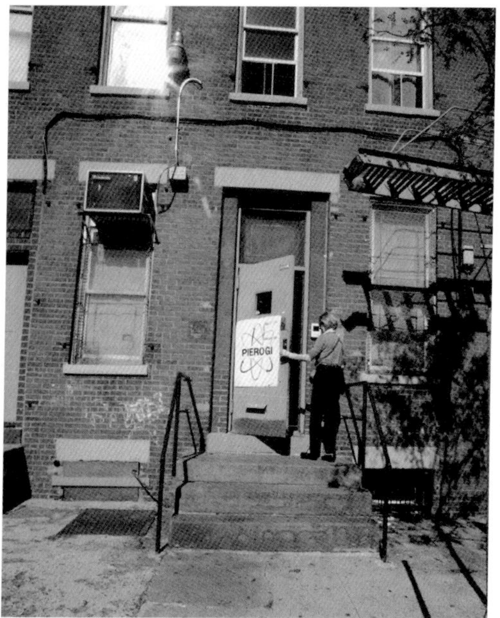

own art work, curating in other spaces, and creative projects such as the biannual journal *Pierogi Press*. Pierogi 2000 has brought him much attention, a benefit to his own reputation, as well as to the artists on file. It has also greatly increased the number of people who want to have their work put into the files and consequently much of Amrhein's time these days is spent looking at new talent.

ADDRESS 167 North 9th Street, Brooklyn, NY 11211 (718 599 2144)
WEBSITE www.pierogi2000.com
OPEN Saturday, Sunday and Monday, 12–6, or call for appointment
SUBWAY Bedford Avenue L, then walk north two blocks

Pierogi 2000

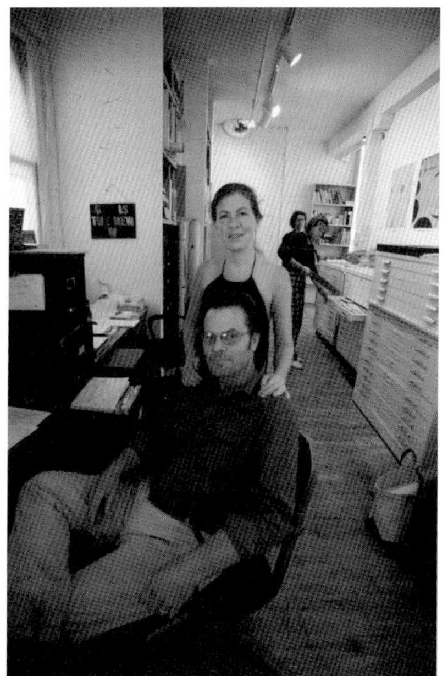

queens

PS1 Contemporary Art Center 9.2

PS1 Contemporary Art Center

What began 27 years ago as a project to utilise space in derelict urban buildings, has become one of the most renowned centres for international contemporary art. Originally founded as The Institute of Art and Urban Resources Inc., this nomadic organisation's purpose was to foster and encourage art exhibitions, performance, and studio spaces outside of the mainstream. It became PS1 when it moved to a permanent location in Long Island City. The name derives from the New York City public-school organisation's democratic appellation system; that is, each school is given the initials PS and a number. Just as American public schools have an egalitarian ethos, so too PS1 is an institution dedicated to educating the public rather than the elite art set.

PS1 has evolved from an organisation with no home to its current megastructure of more than 100,000 square feet, one of the largest centres for contemporary art in the world in terms of programmable space. Unlike other huge institutions, PS1 has no permanent collection, but relies on the resourcefulness of its curators to keep the space full. At any one time a visitor might stumble upon a large group theme show, an installation by a Japanese artist, or a performance by a young live-art entertainer. What the visitor can be sure of is that whatever they experience, it will be of a very high standard; both edge and eclectic.

PS1's staff curators are assisted through their Herculean programming task by a prestigious line up of guest curators from around the globe. The programme that relaunched the space after a three-year makeover was devised by PS1's director Alana Heiss, with Klaus Biesenbach, Kazue Kobata, and Michael Tarantino. Biesenbach is the latest *Wunderkind* to emerge from Germany and his work with the 1998 Berlin Biennale, along with the PS1 project, has established him as one of the art world's big players. Kobata and Tarantino, from Japan and the US respectively, repre-

PS1 Contemporary Art Center

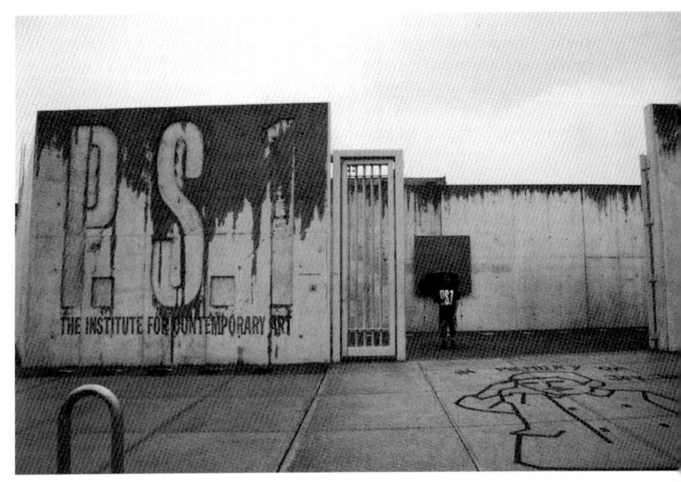

sent a more established generation of renowned curators. Their ambitious programme included a recreation of PS1's first-ever 1976 exhibition. The regular exhibition programme is usually previewed on Sunday afternoons when New York's art glitterati view new works, socialise, drink beer and generally have a good time with up-and-coming artists, critics and anyone else who happens across this happening happening.

While the shape of PS1 has certainly changed, its director never has. Alanna Heiss started this ambitious programme in 1971, and she remains its guiding beacon. In fact, PS1's variety mirrors her own personality. The path that took Heiss to directing America's largest contemporary art space previously saw her selling used cars, teaching religion, and working as a criminologist. It is perhaps fitting that Heiss was one of the first to host exhibitions in alternative spaces. Organising shows in such unlikely places as under the Brooklyn Bridge with then unknown artists including Carl Andre, Phillip Glass, and Sol LeWitt, Heiss' knack for the unpredictable represents what it takes to run PS1.

The Center came of age in 1999 when it officially became part of the New York *uber*-art-power, the Museum of Modern Art. The benefits of this merger remain to be seen. Although financially it is obvious that their bonding will benefit and ensure the future of PS1, the jury is still out as to whether or not the Center's alignment with the establishment will decrease the innovative kudos for which it is celebrated.

ADDRESS 22–25 Jackson Avenue at 46th Avenue, Long Island City, Queens, NY 11101 (718 784 2084)
WEBSITE www.ps1.org
HOURS Wednesday to Sunday, 12.00–18.00
SUBWAY 23rd Street Jackson Avenue, E, F

PS1 Contemporary Art Center

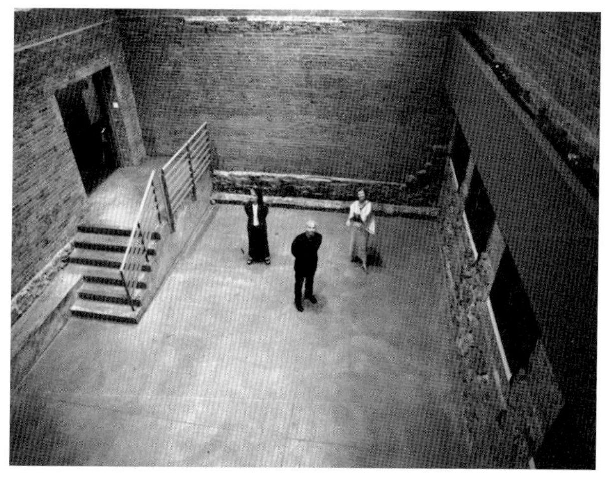

index

Index

Index

index of artists

Index of Artists

Index of Artists

Index of Artists